A Silvey-Jex

BAD TASTE BOOK

To ....

From ....

ISBN 0 907 280 12 9

BY ALL THAT'S HOLY

Published in Great Britain by Silvey-Jex Publications

Printed in England by Merlin Colour Printers, Canvey Island, Essex.

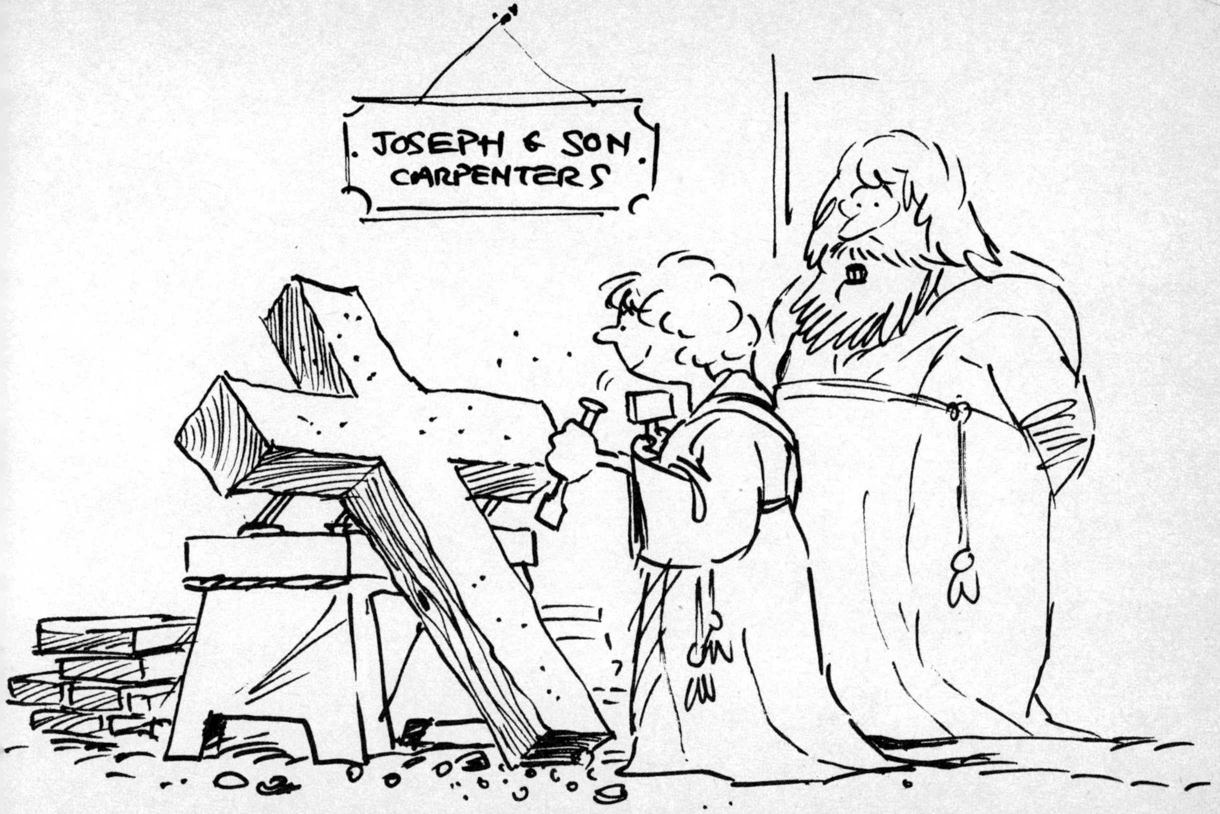
JOSEPH & SON
CARPENTERS

"Why can't you make pipe racks like other kids?"

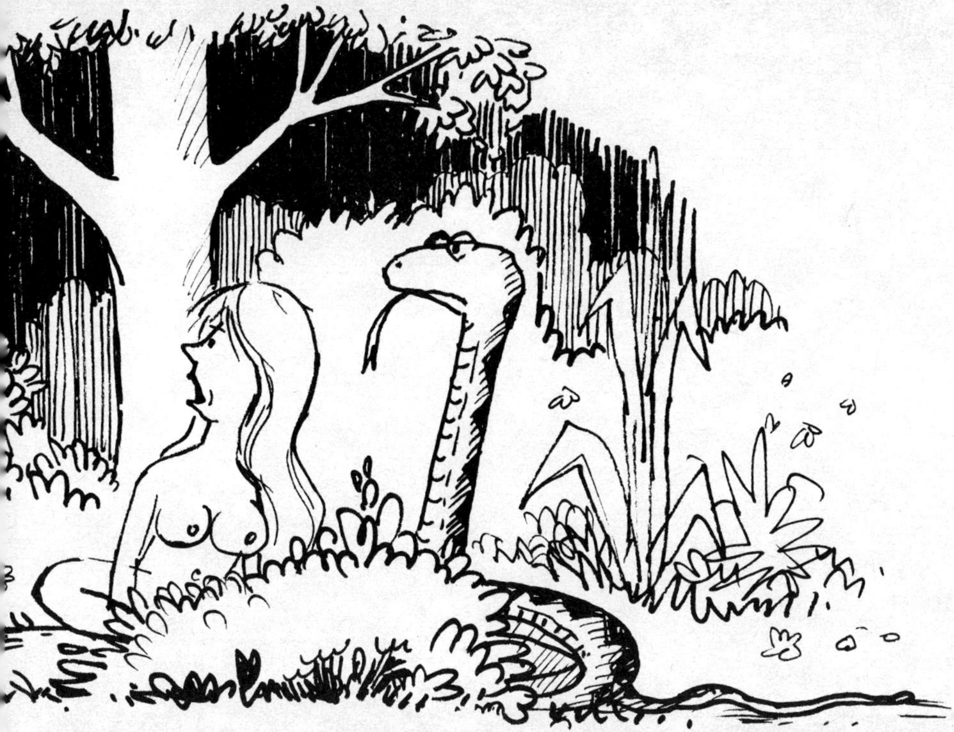

"Would you believe it . . . I tempt him with an apple and it gives him diarrhoea"

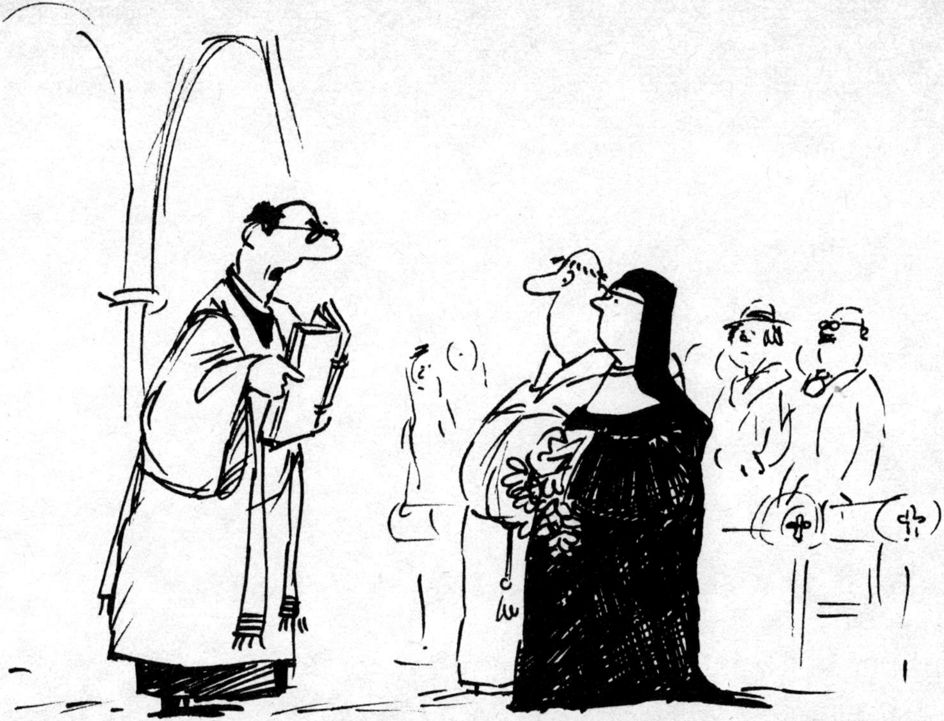

"There's something you two have kept from me isn't there?"

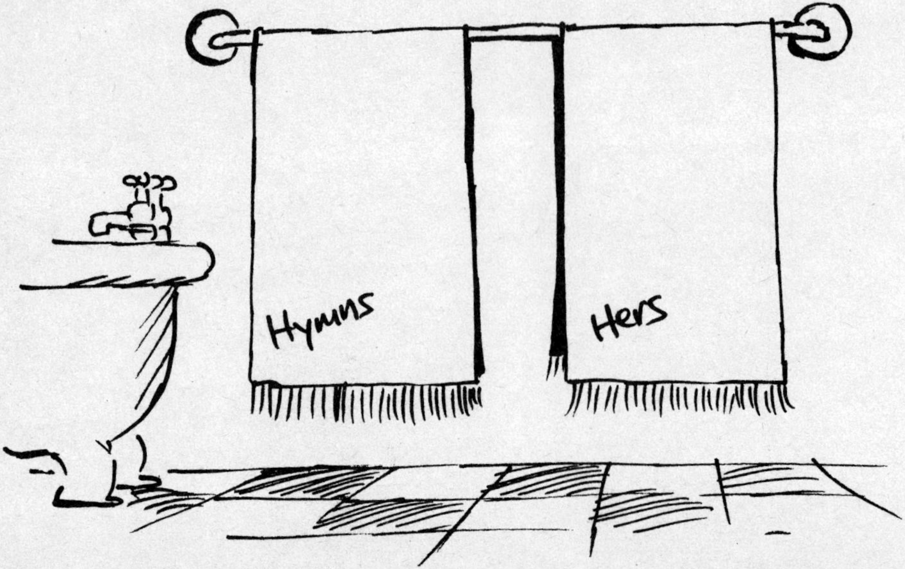
Hymns
Hers

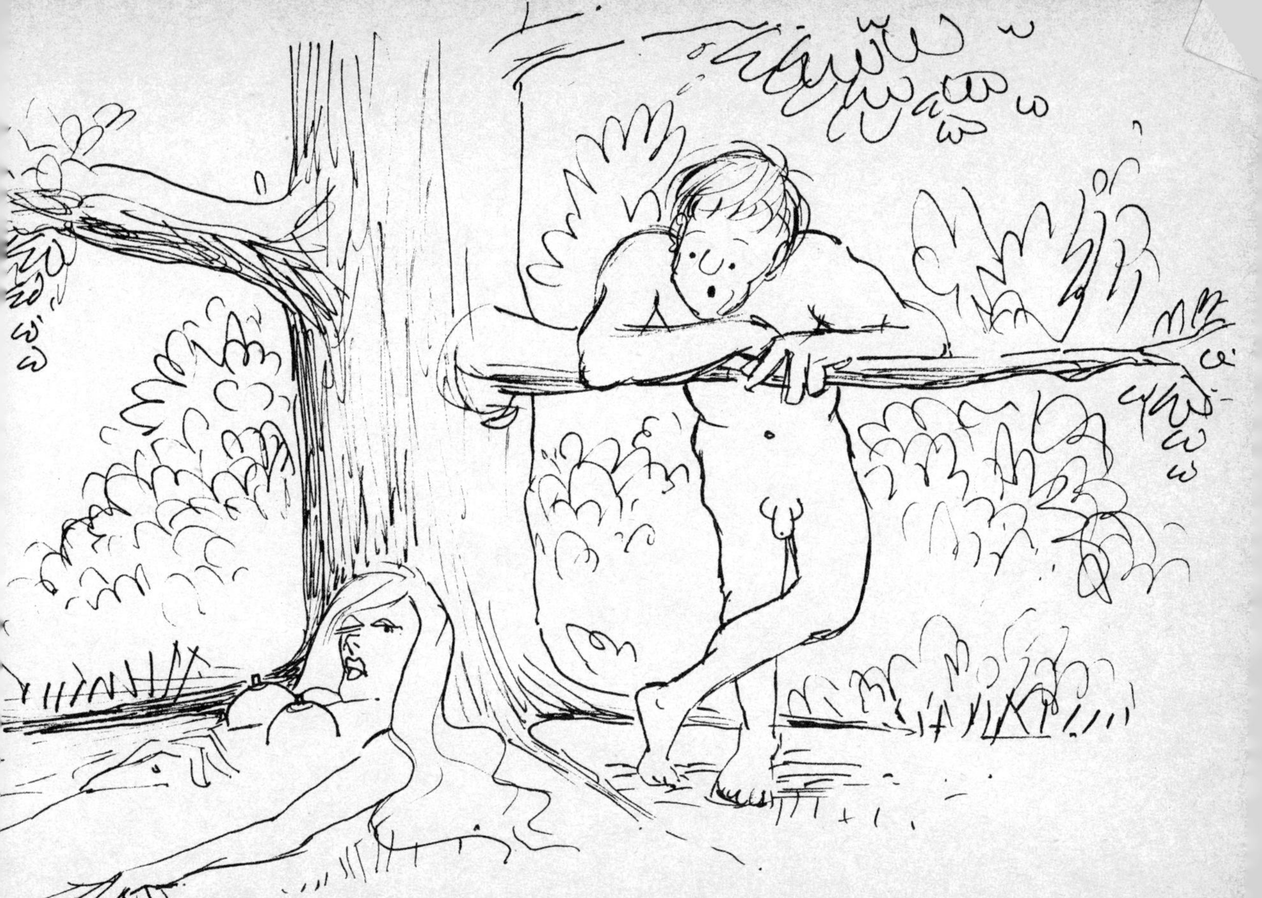

"Fancy a bit of original sin?"

"The Bishop's here"

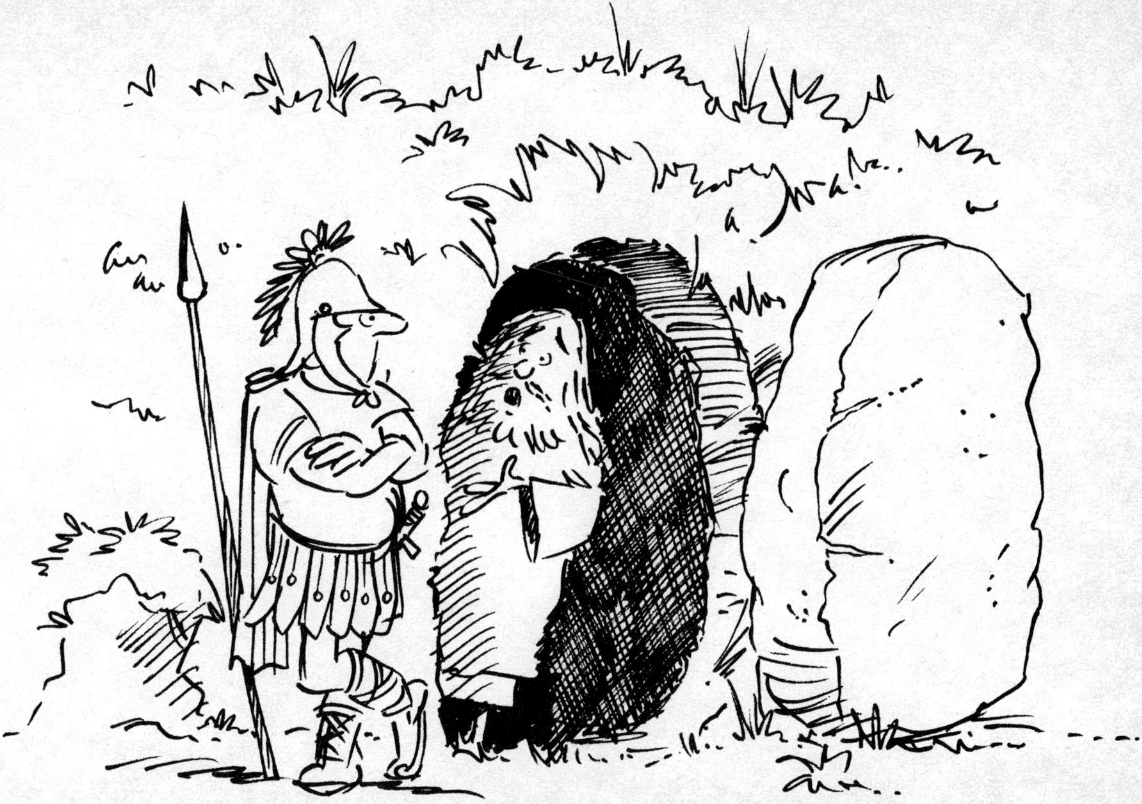

"I tell you he's not in here – and that's gospel"

"All his life he'd been waiting for a sign – and now this"

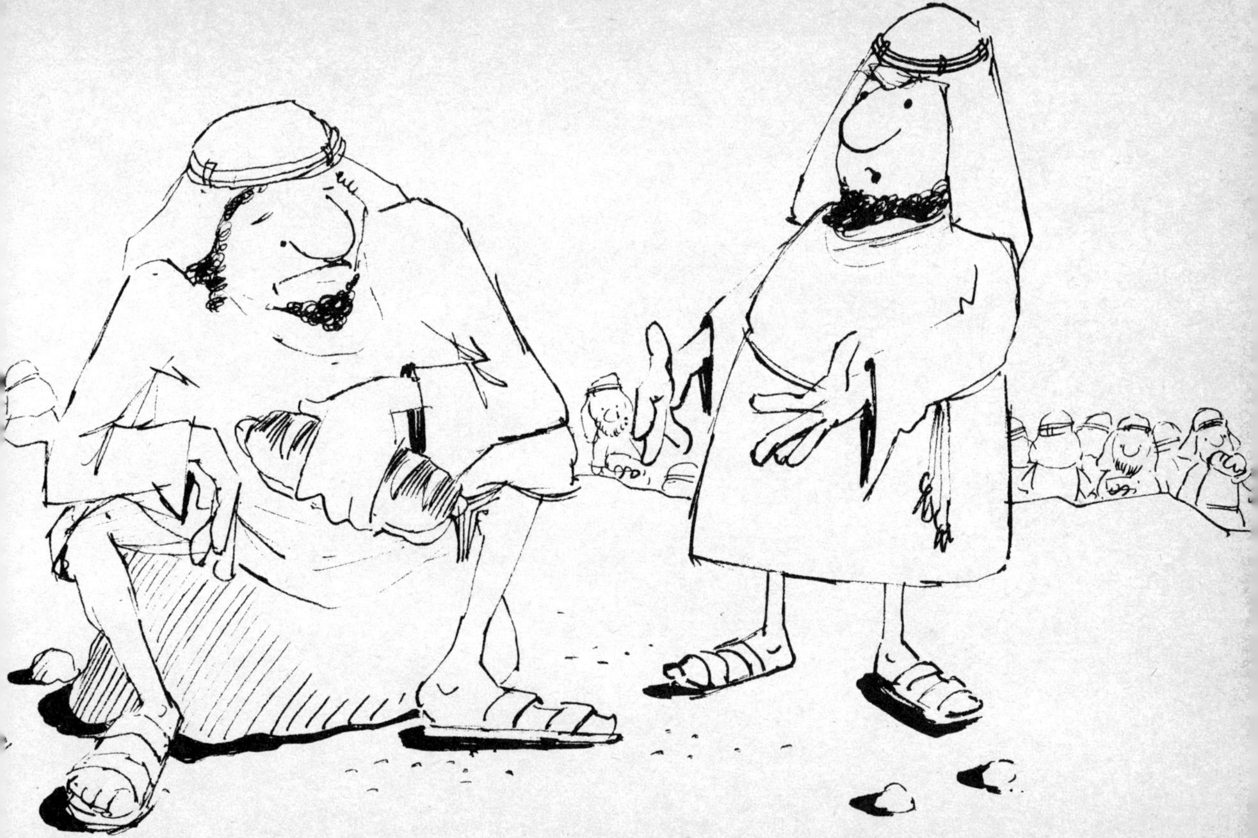

"So it's sardine sandwiches again – what else do you expect with fishes and loaves?"

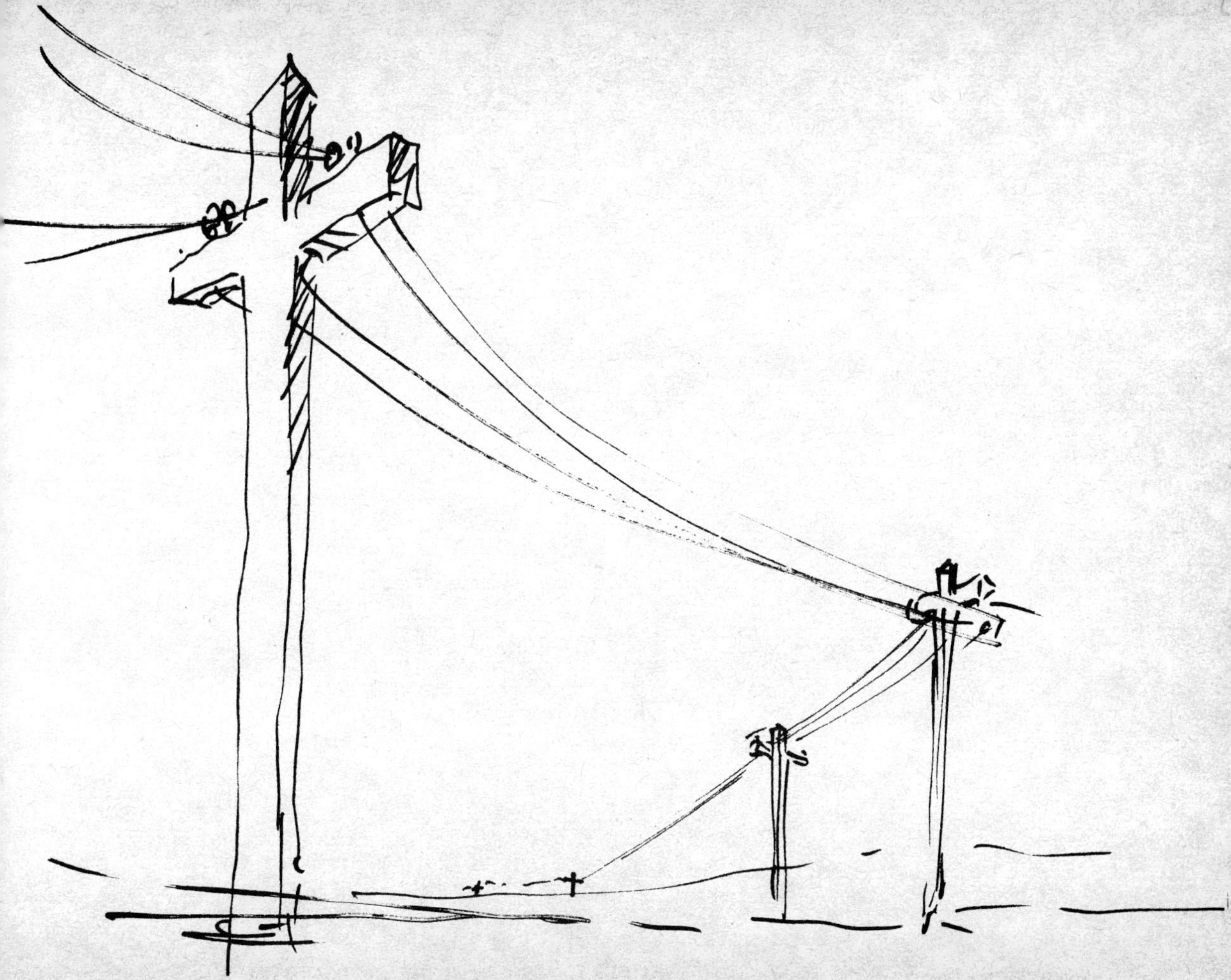

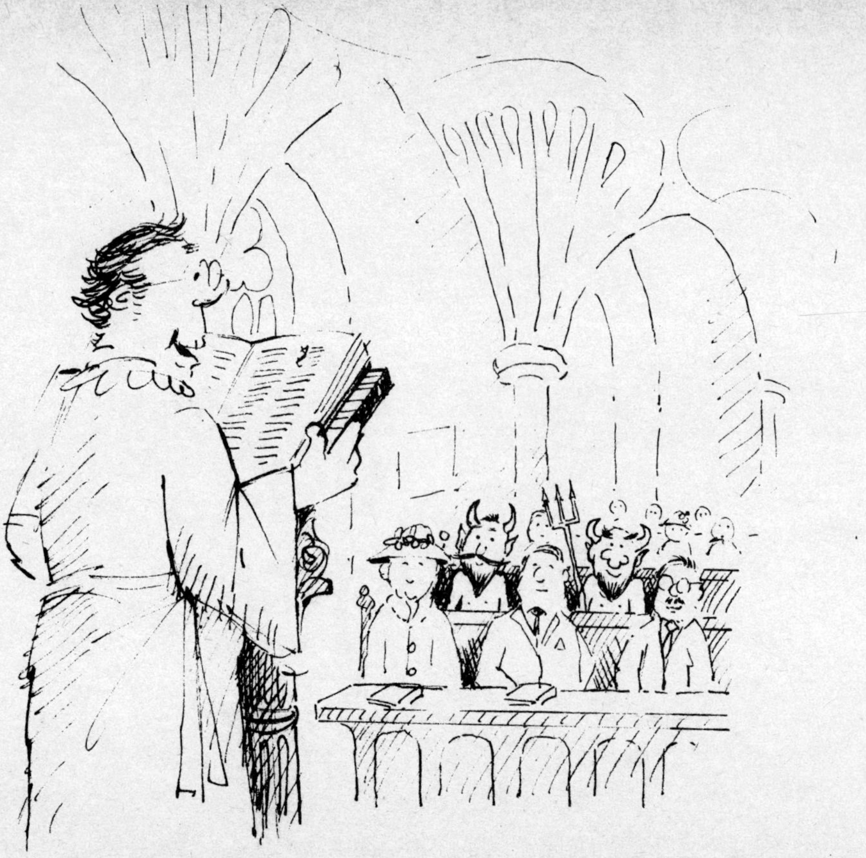

"I see we have some new faces with us today"

"He's the image of his father"

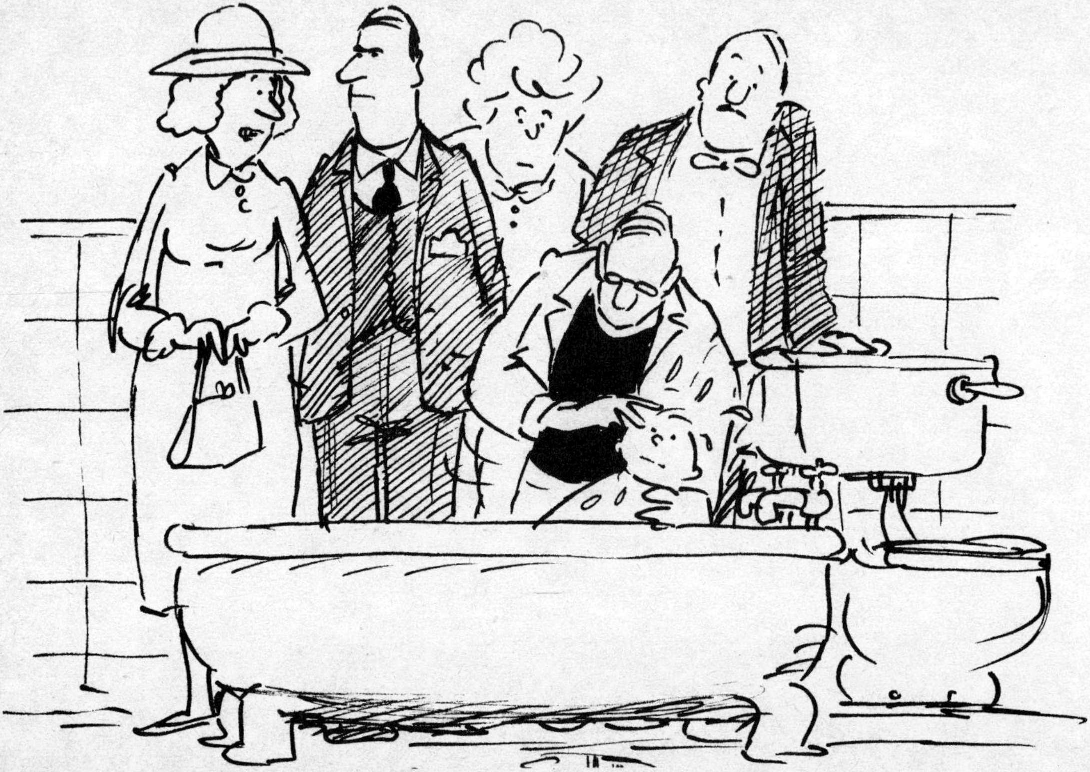

"Well I thought a Christening in the Vicarage would be nice . . . but this . . ."

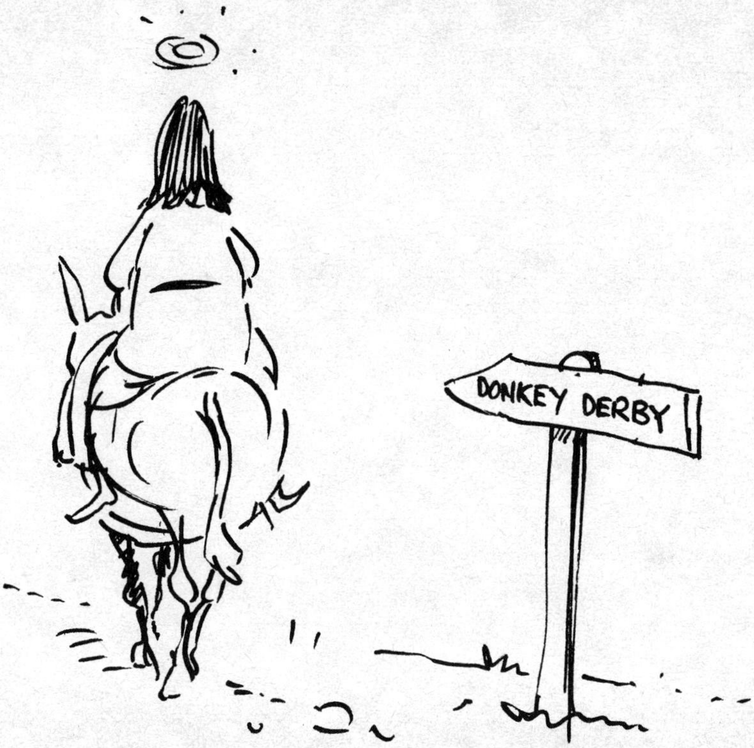
DONKEY DERBY

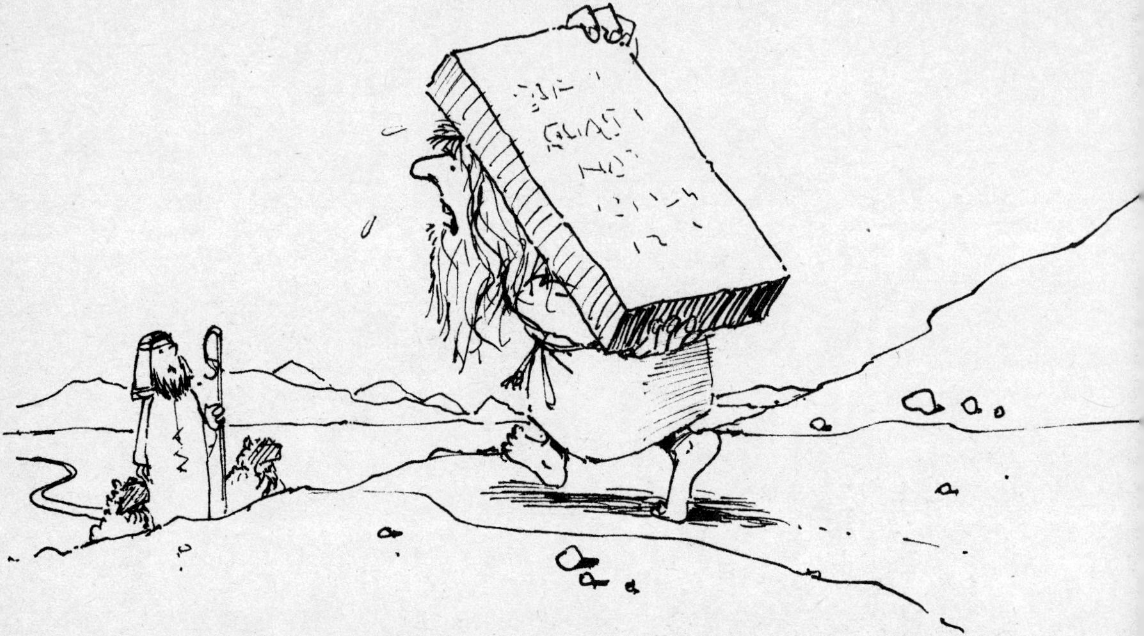

"There's another nine of these bloody things up there"

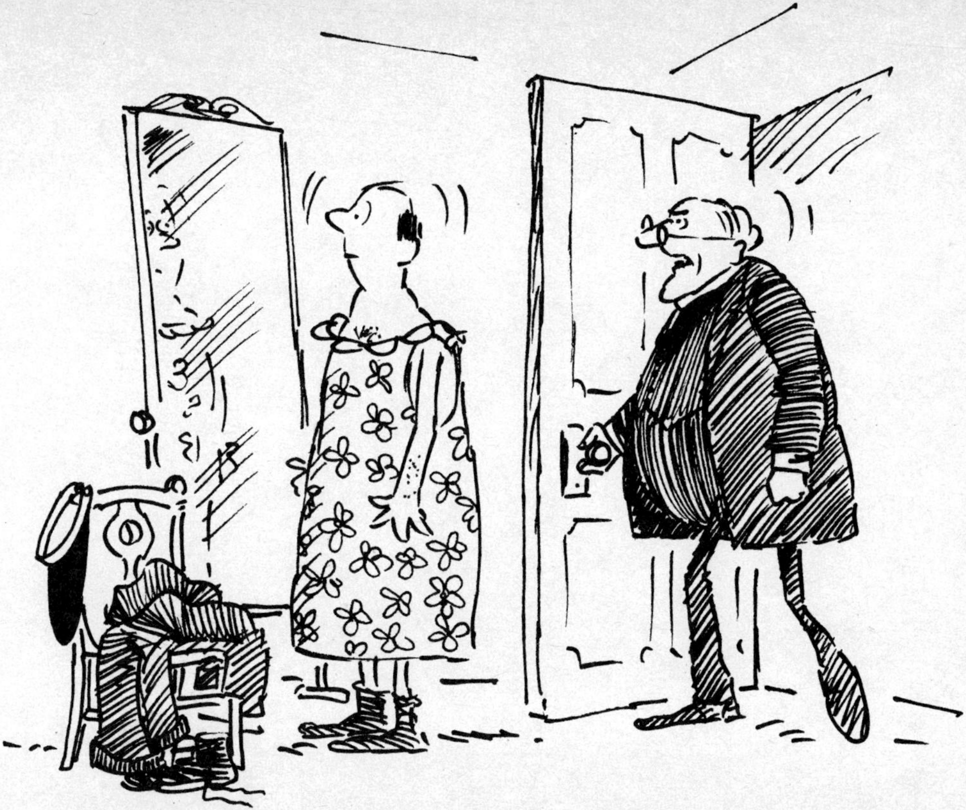

"Consider yourself de-frocked"

"Pork pies! oy vey! that's the Last Supper you cater for"

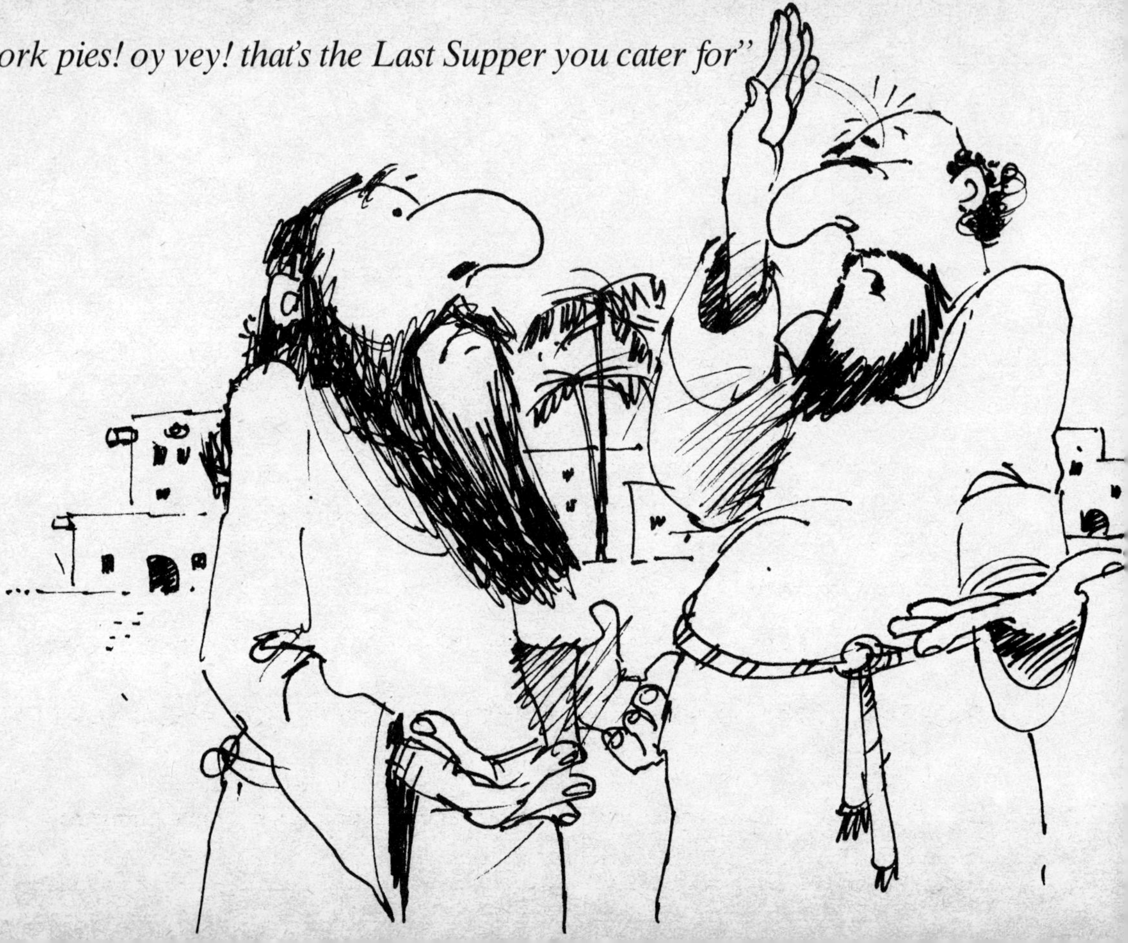

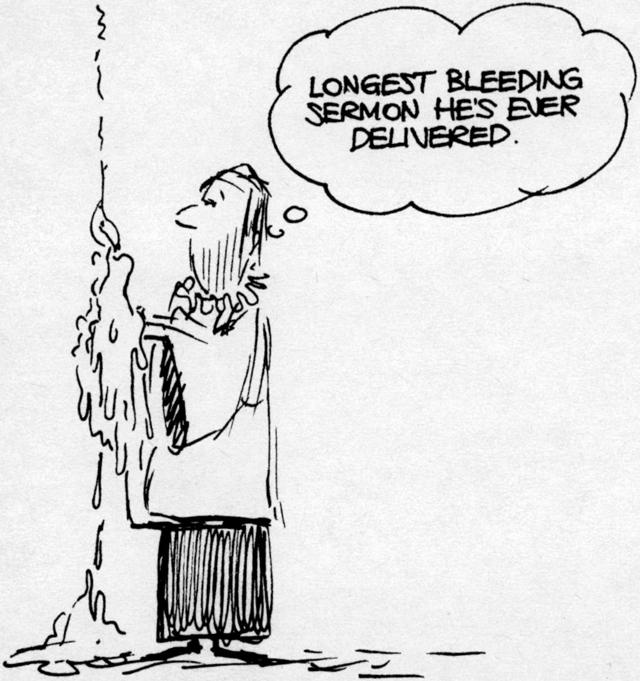
LONGEST BLEEDING SERMON HE'S EVER DELIVERED.

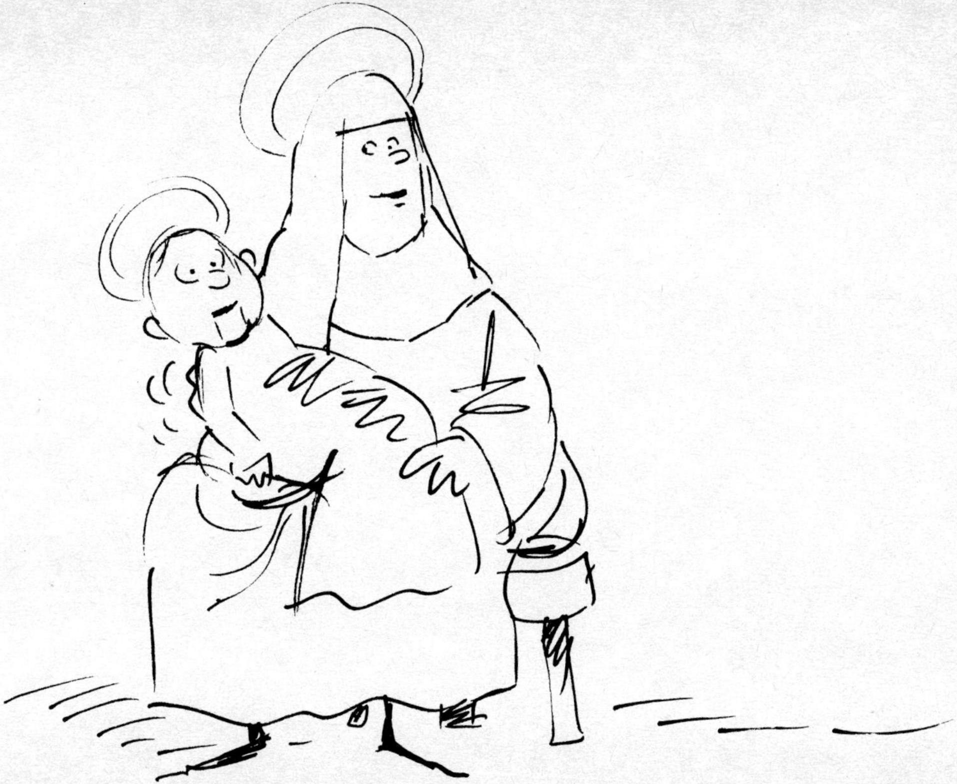

"A gottle of geer – a gottle of geer"

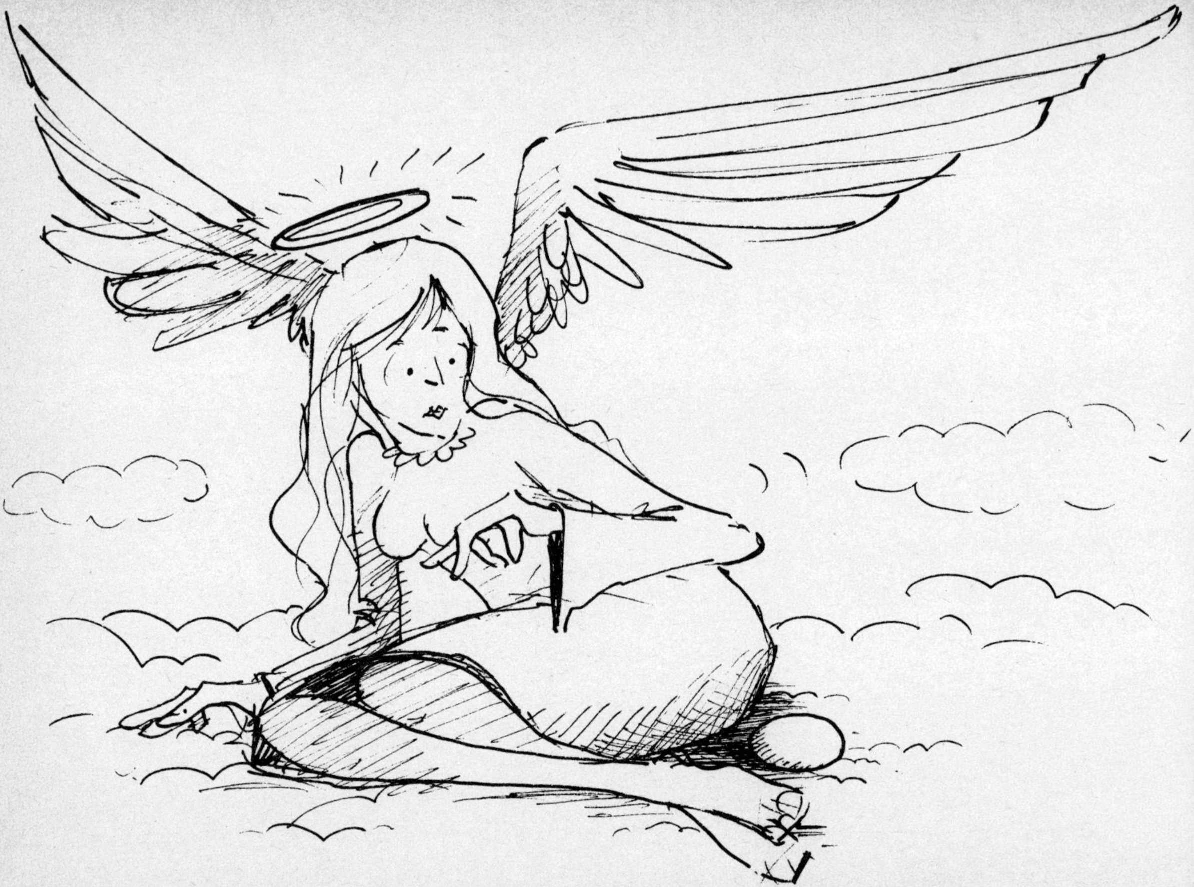

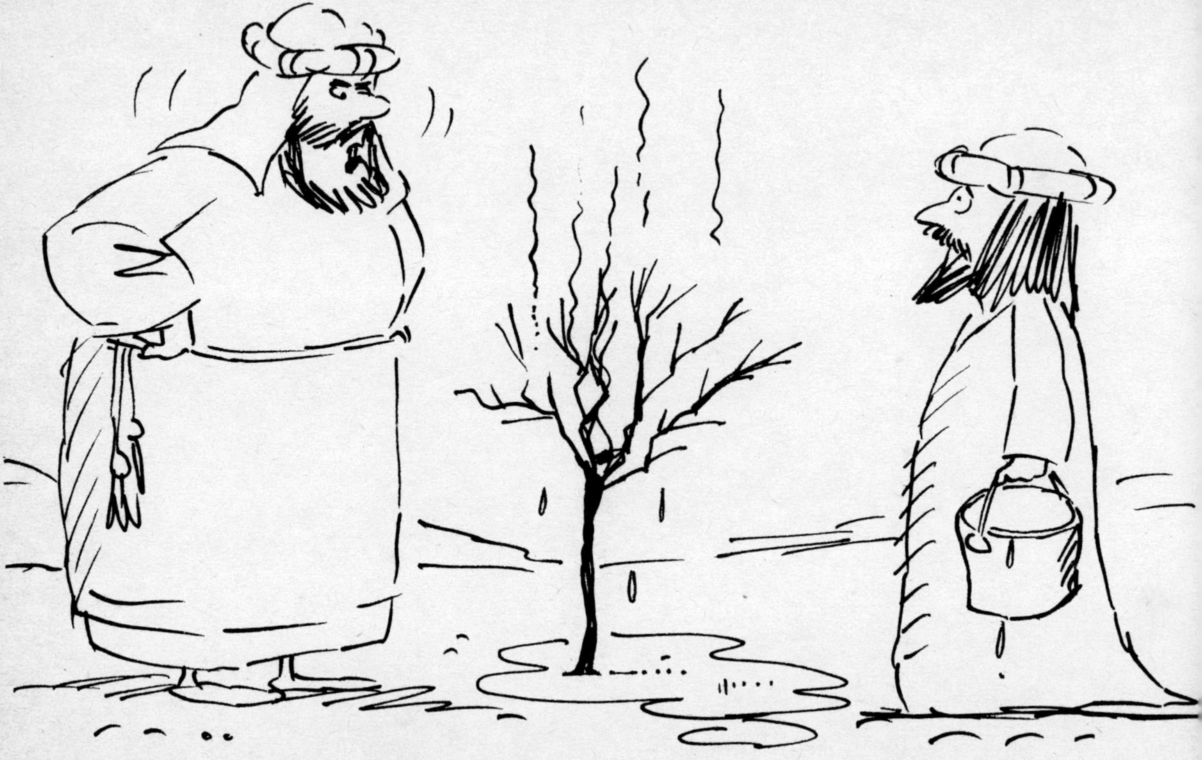

"It was supposed *to be burning you twit"*

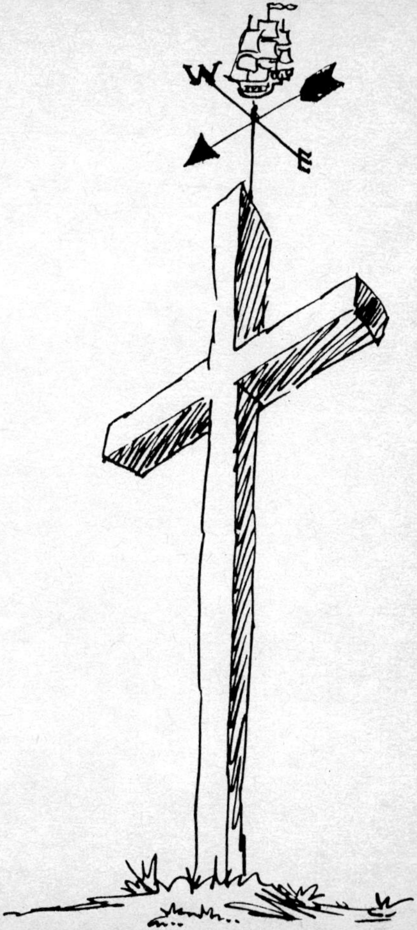
W
E

"I think I've got Religion"

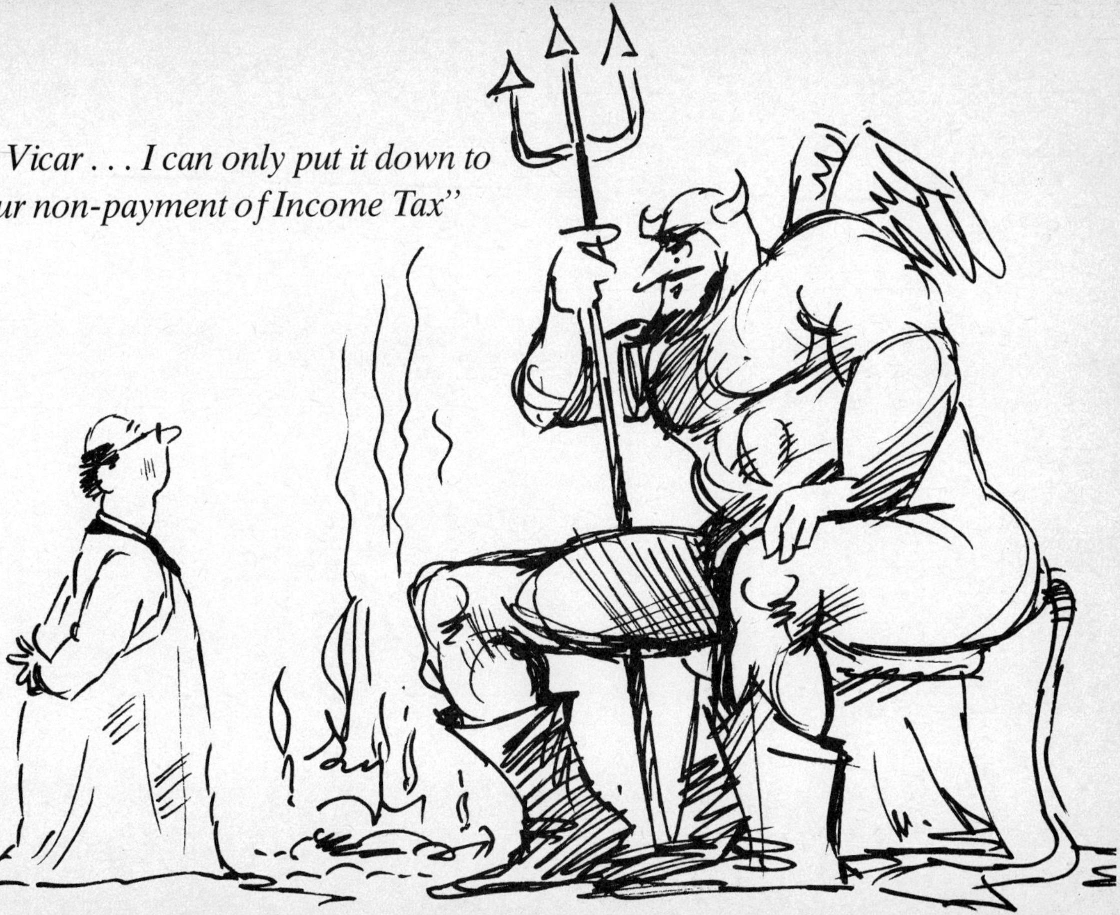

"Well Vicar . . . I can only put it down to your non-payment of Income Tax"

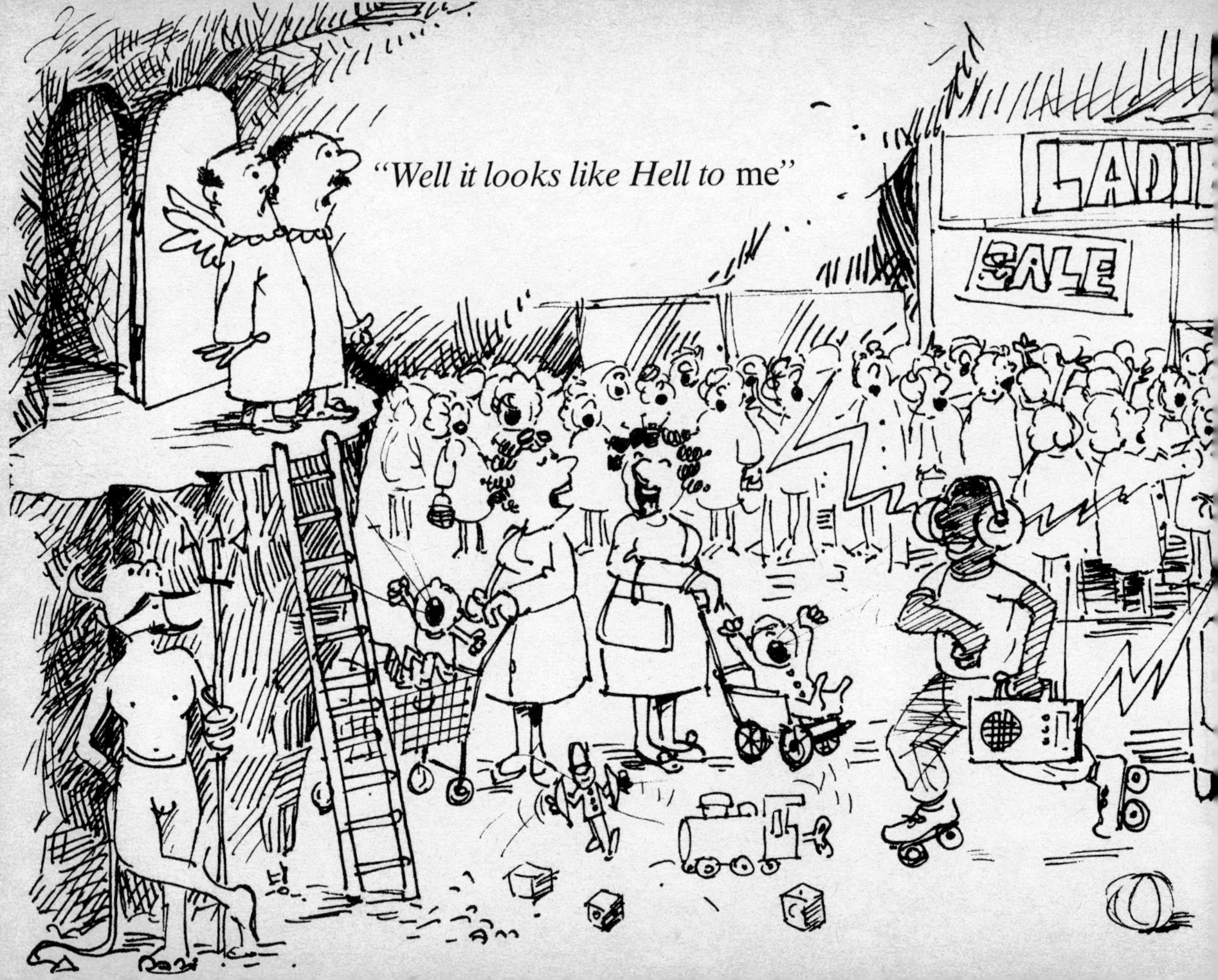
LADI
SALE
"Well it looks like Hell to me"

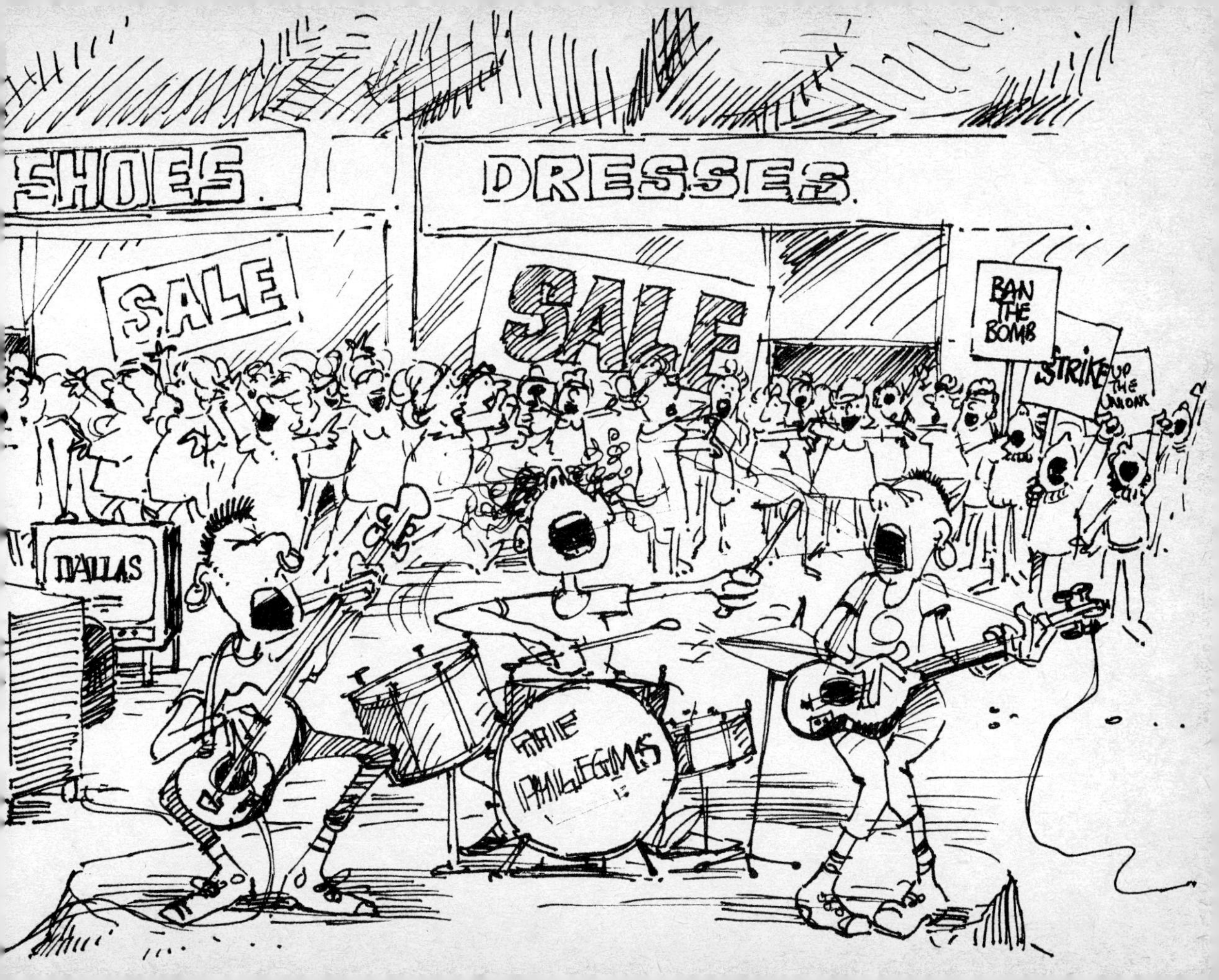
SHOES
DRESSES
SALE
SALE
BAN THE BOMB
STRIKE
UP THE UNION
DALLAS
THE PHLEGMS

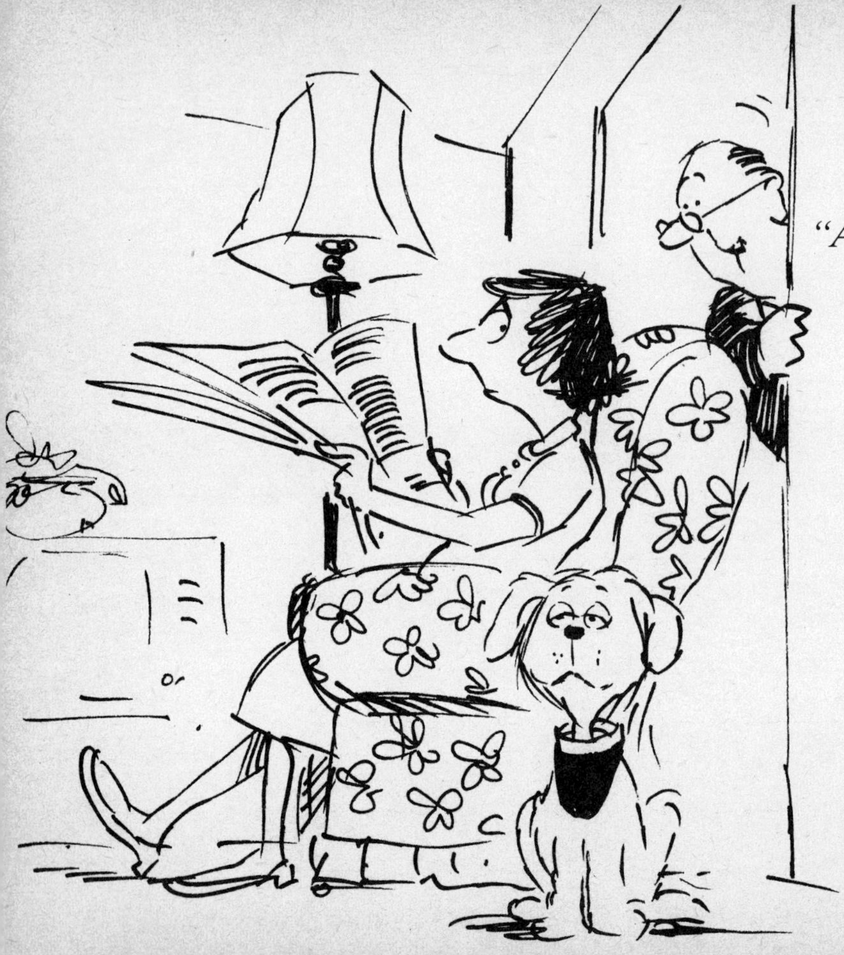

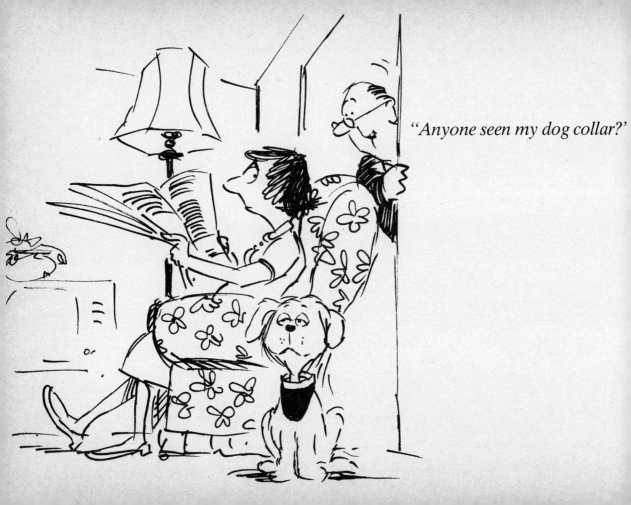

"Anyone seen my dog collar?'

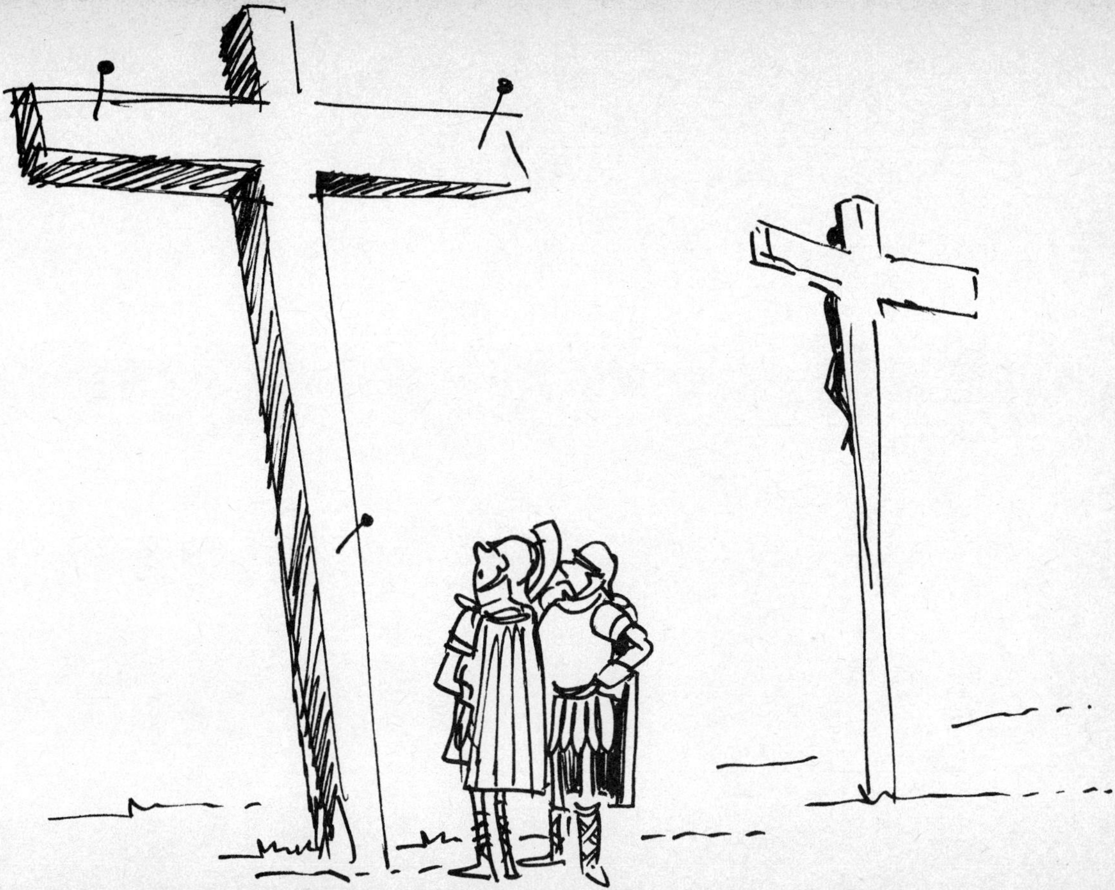

. . ."*and you say he was here when you went to lunch?*"

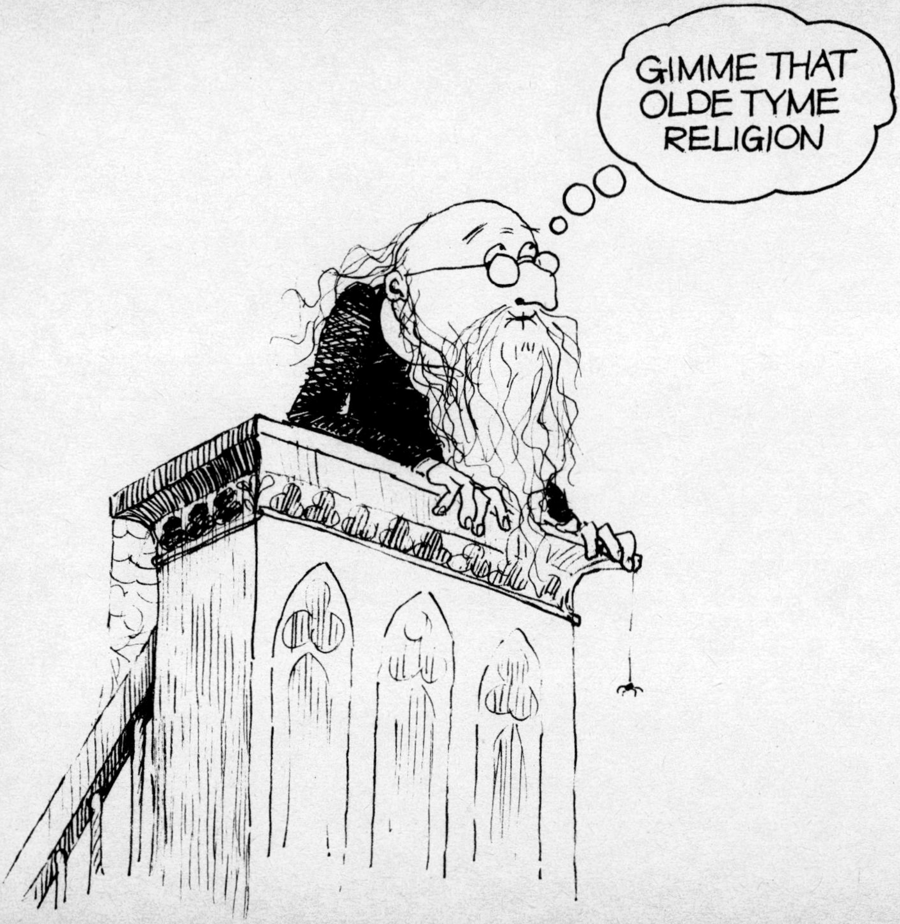
GIMME THAT OLDE TYME RELIGION

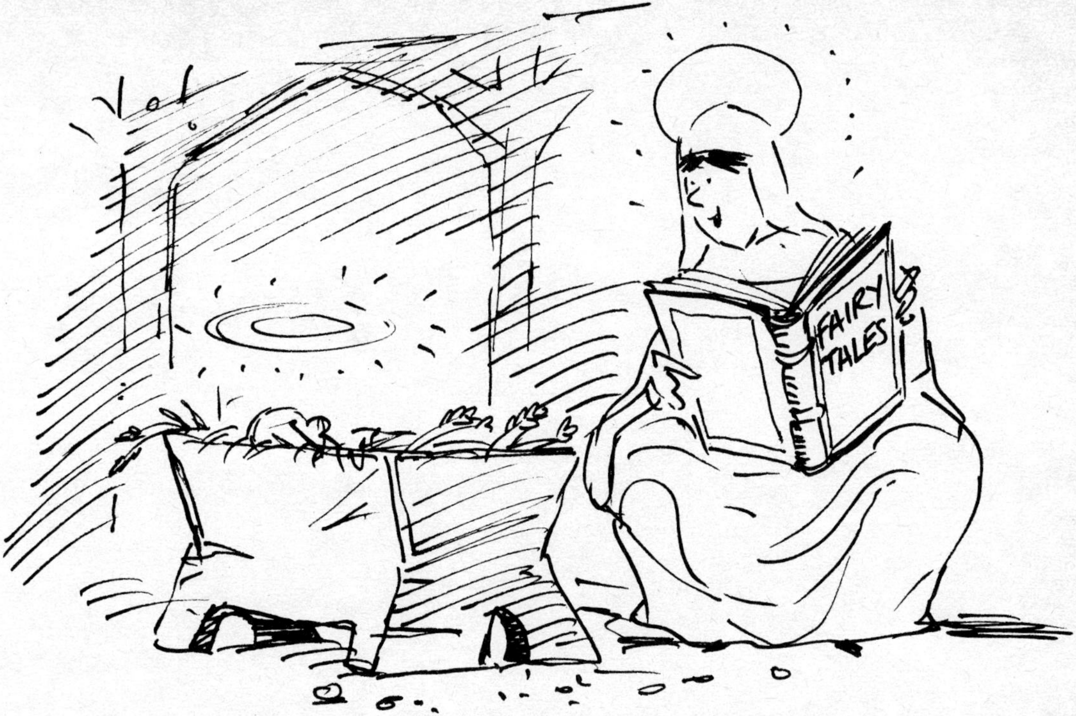
FAIRY TALES

"One more story – then you must put your light off"

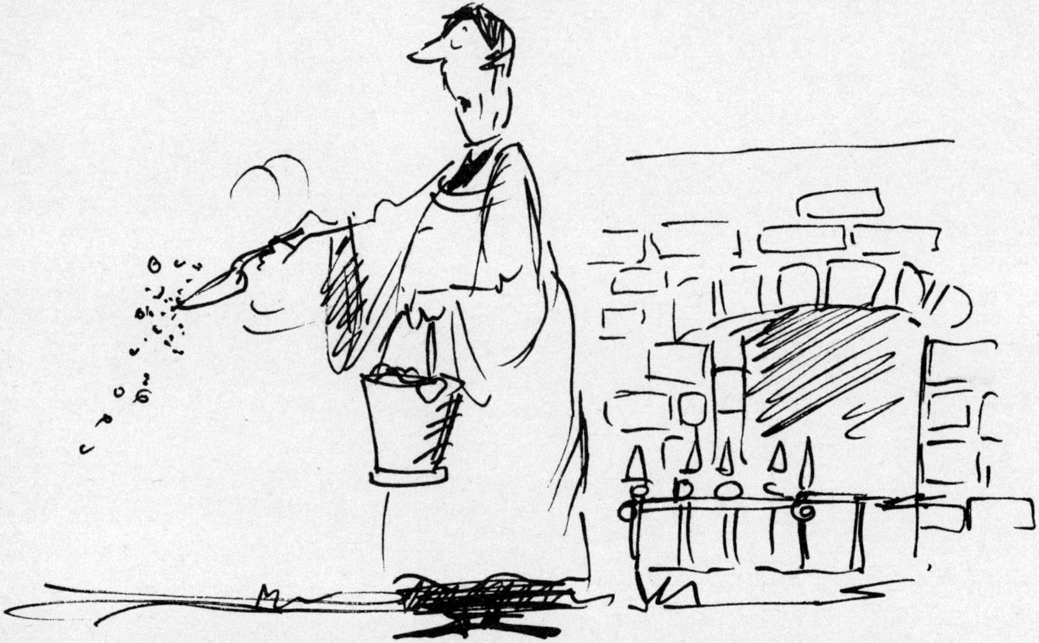

"Ashes to ashes . . ."

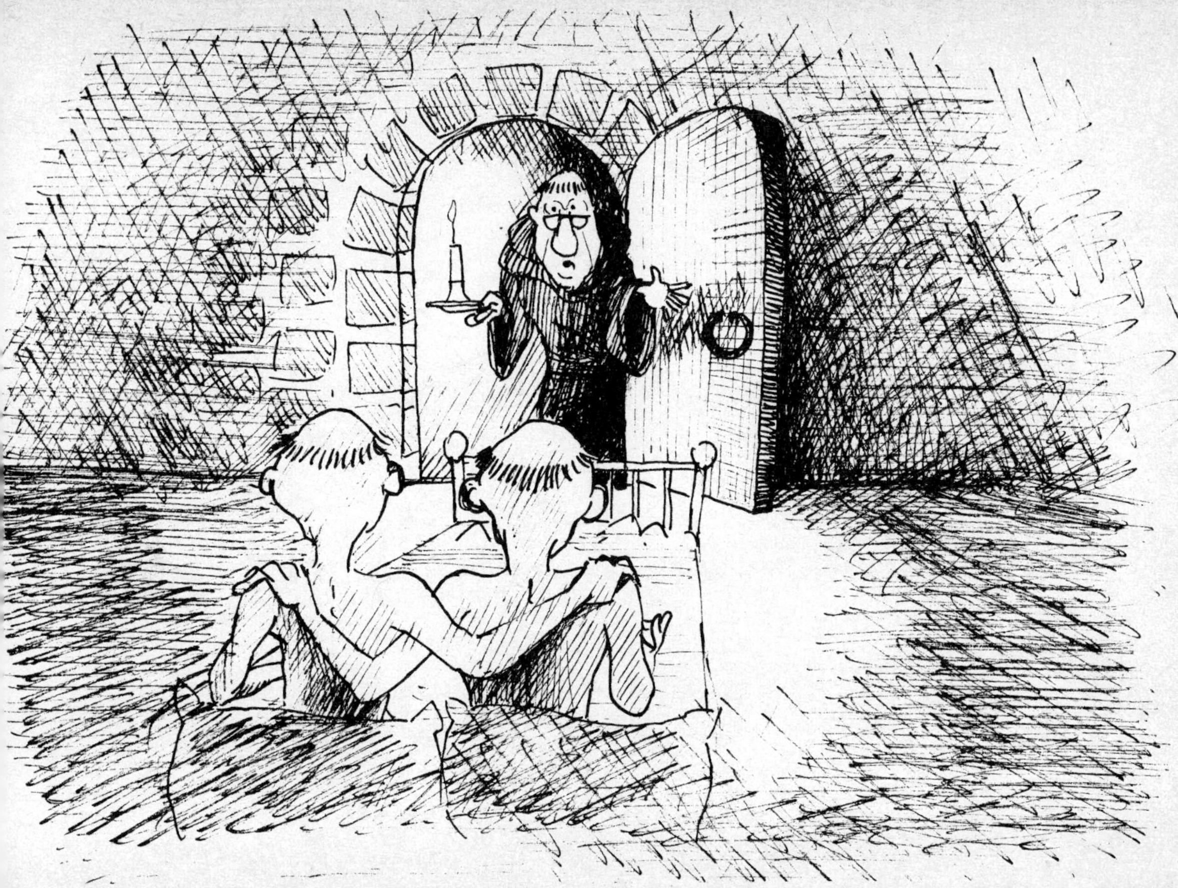

"Stop that Brotherly love you two"

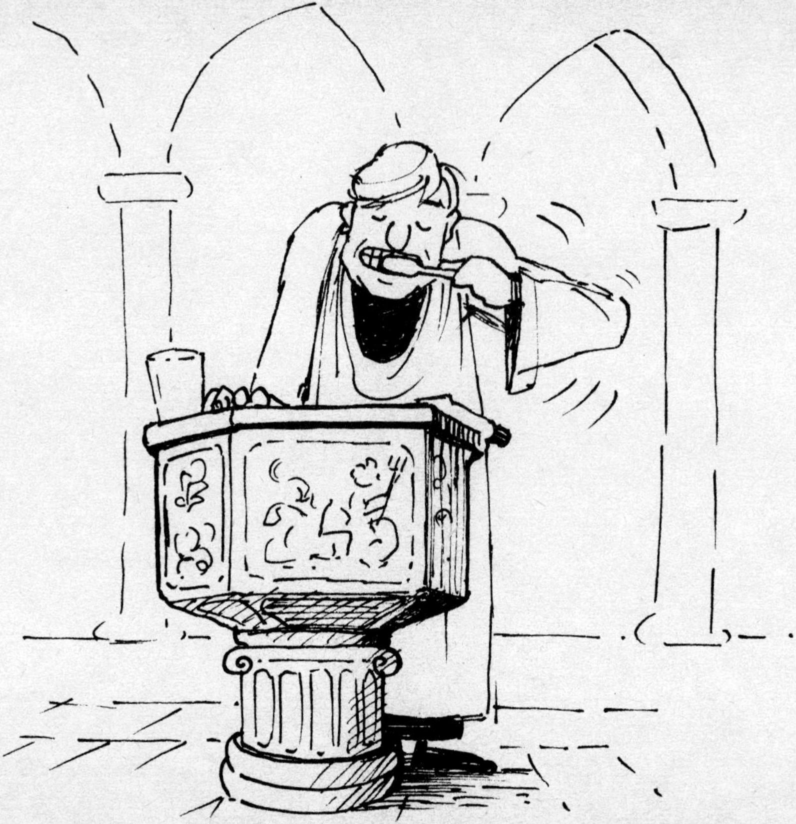

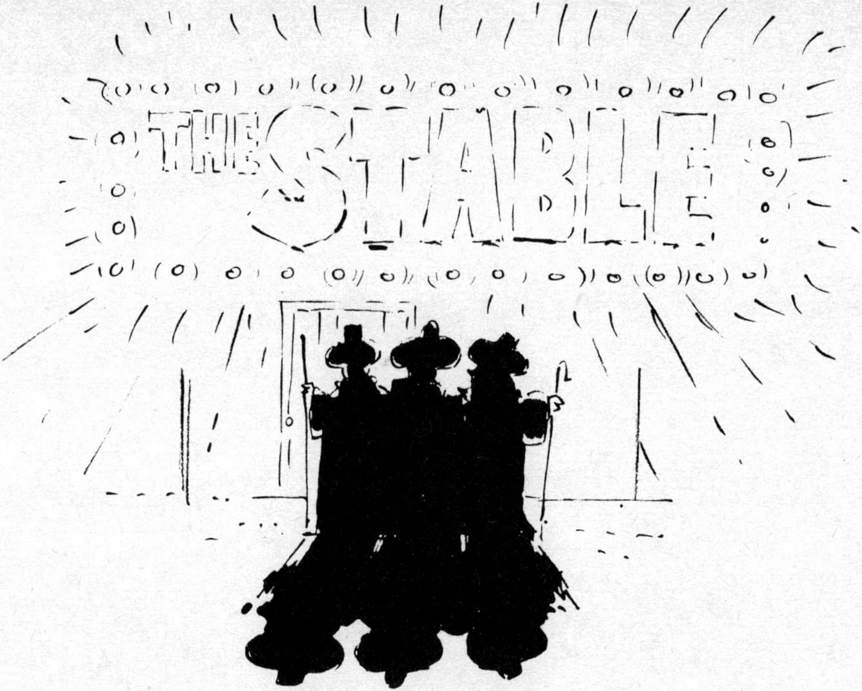
THE STABLE

"Well . . . this must be it"

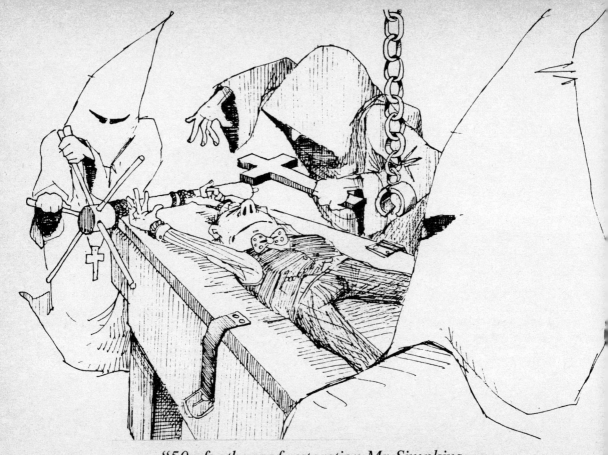

"50p for the roof restoration Mr. Simpkins
– or the Holy Mother Church pulls out another toenail"

"For what you are about to receive"

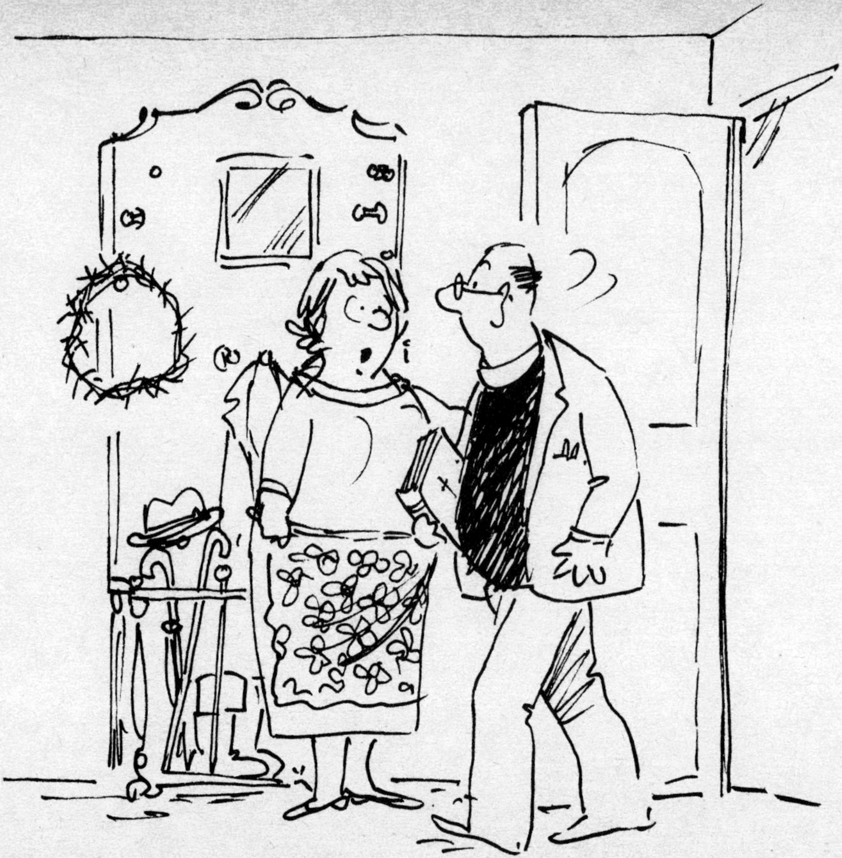

"Hello Henry, we've got a visitor"

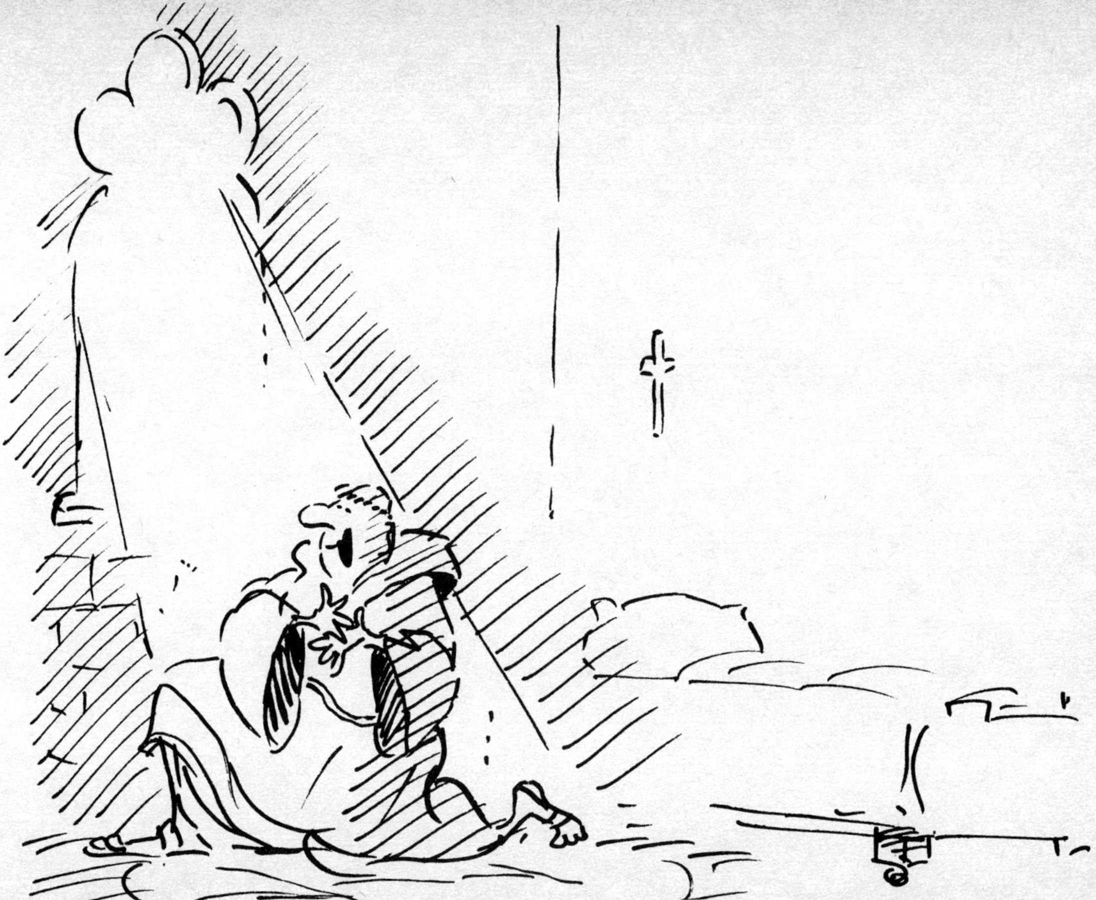

"I'd walk a million miles for one of your smiles . . ."

"... and God bless Mummy, Uncle Jack and Auntie Harriet ..."

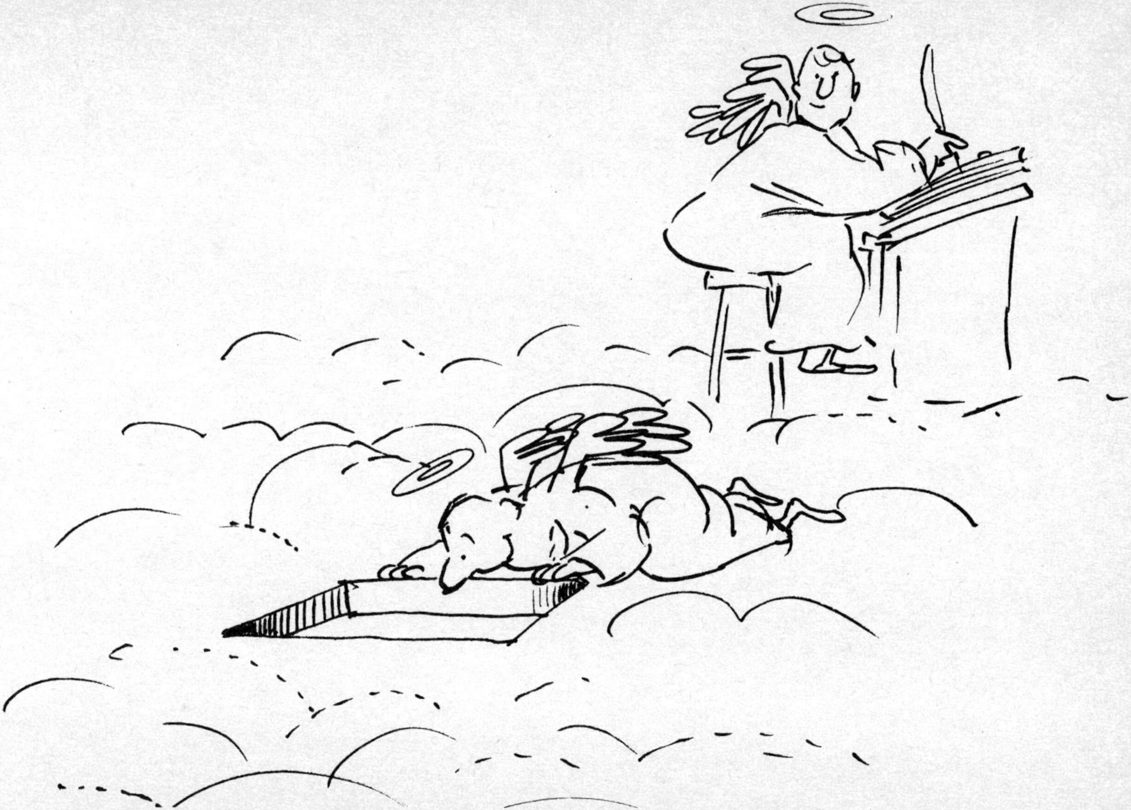

"Get ready for old Mr. Hardcastle – he's in bed with his nurse again"

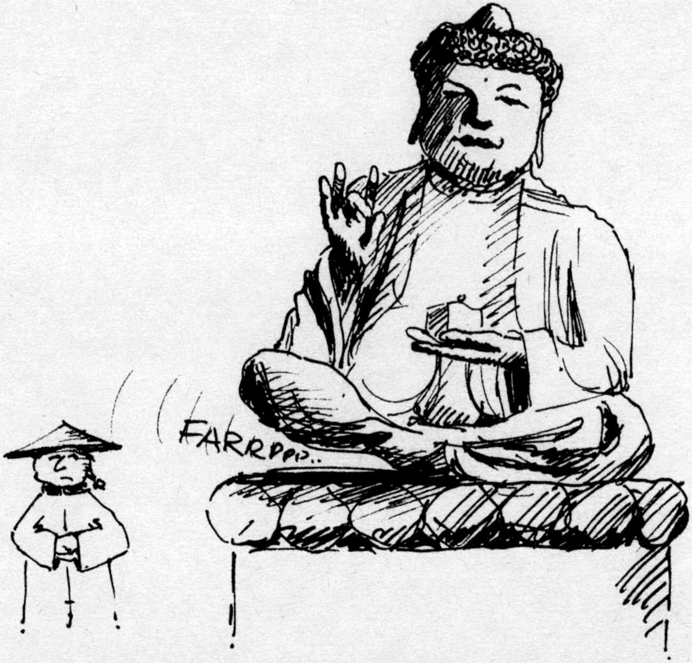
FARRPPP..

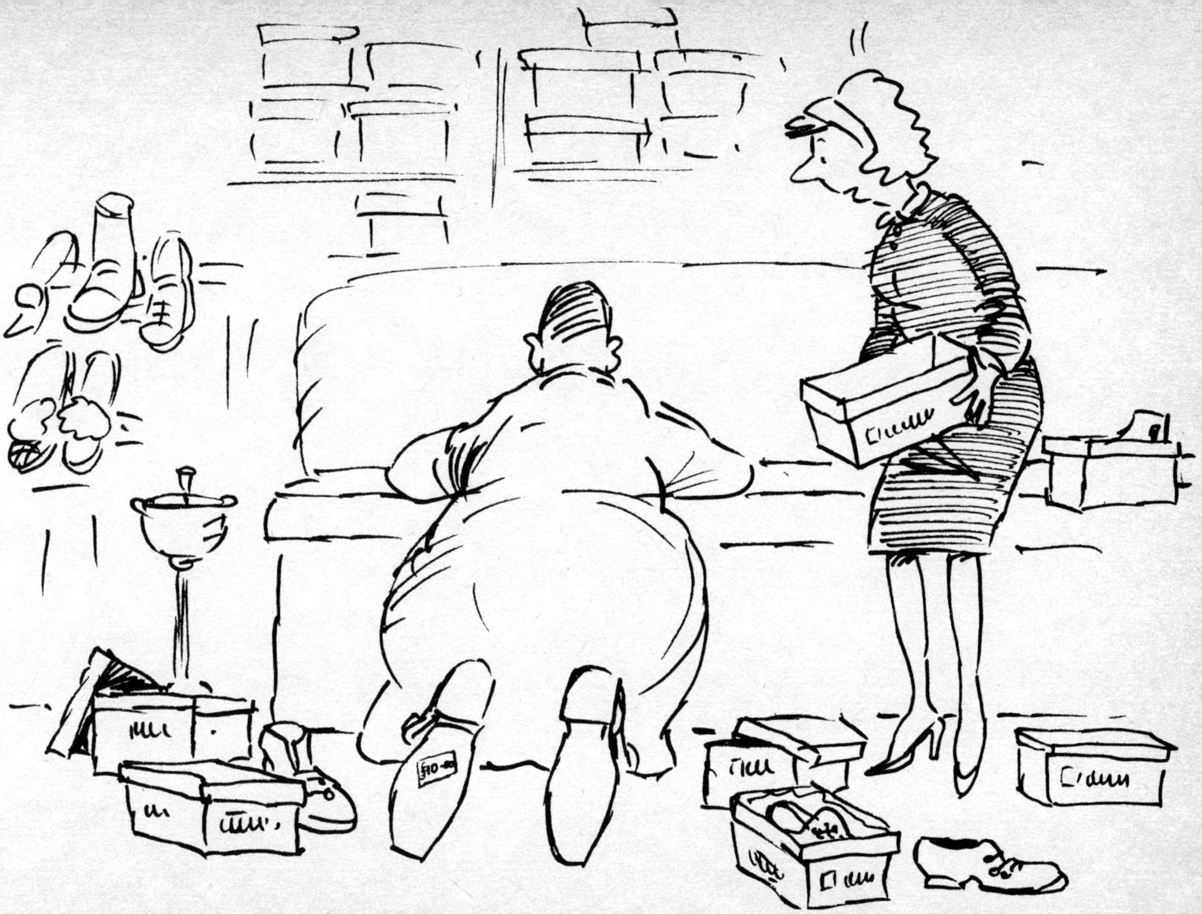

"Well Bishop . . . how do they *feel?"*

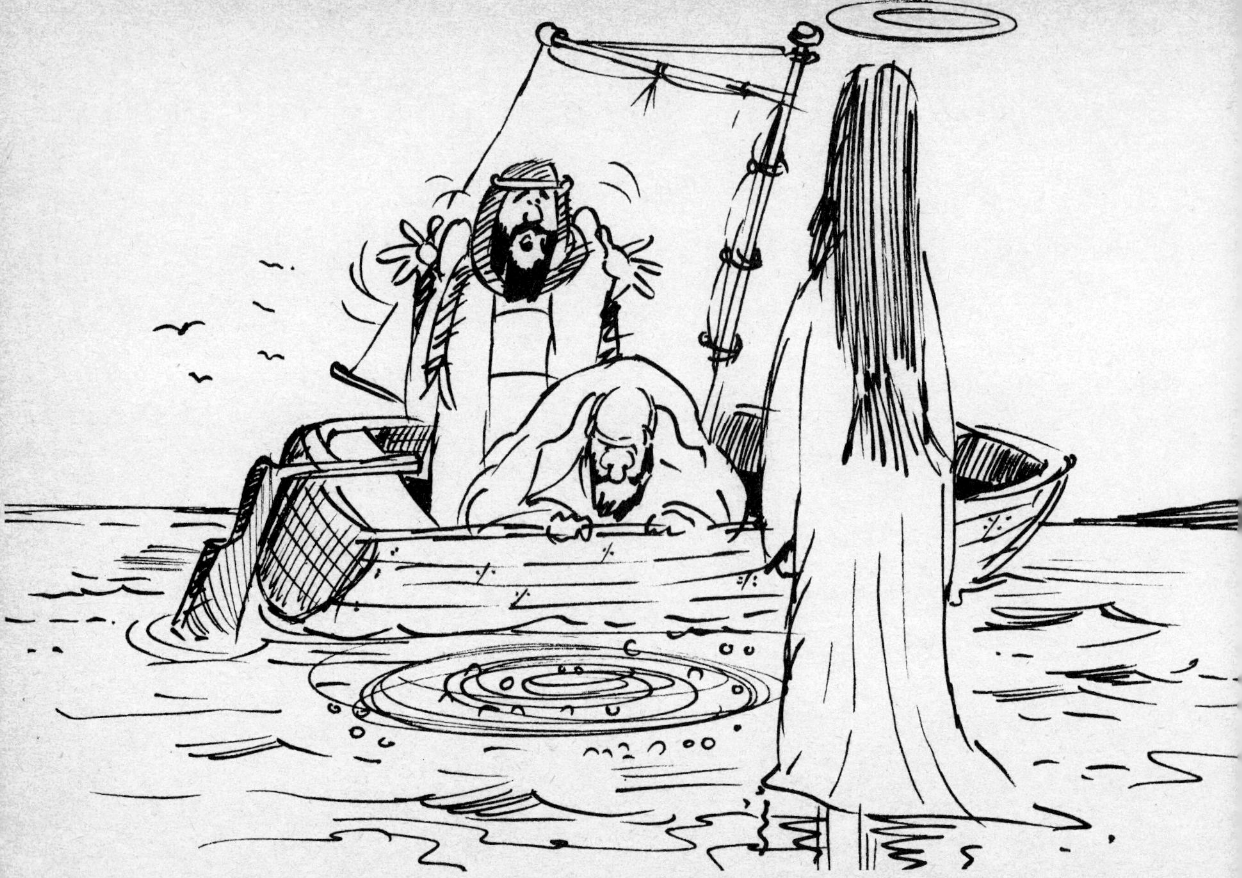

"I think he was coming to shake hands with you"

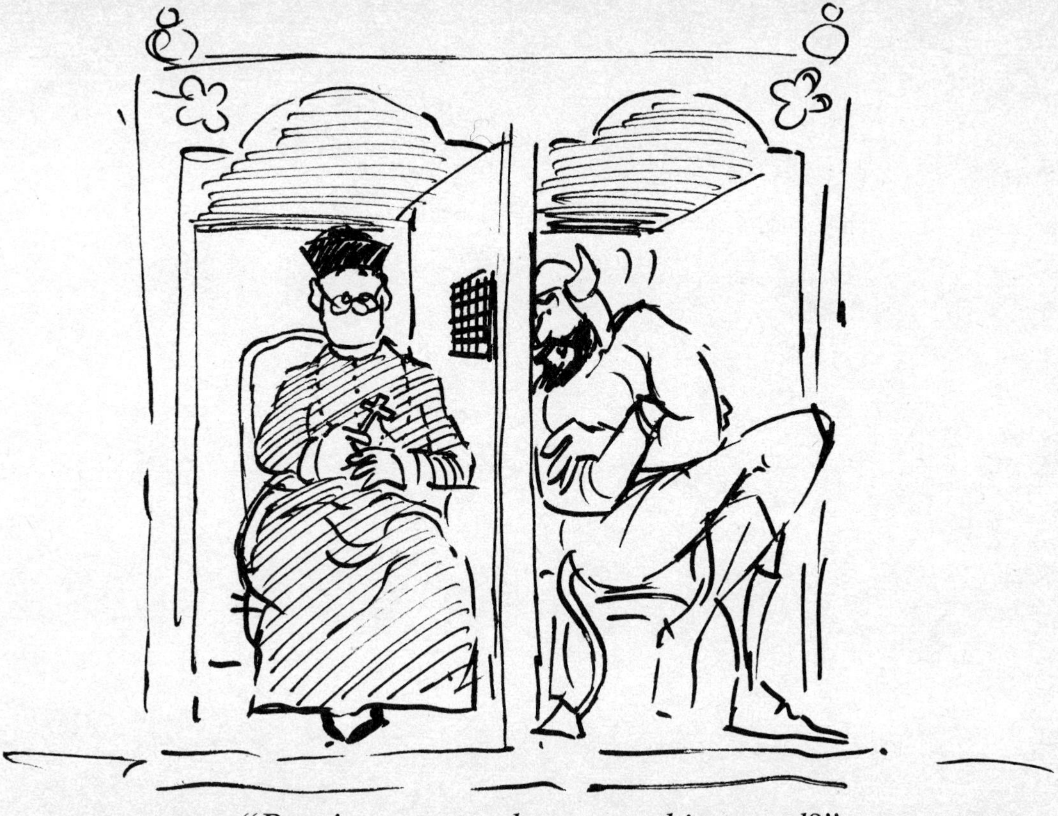

"Pssst! . . . want to hear something good?"

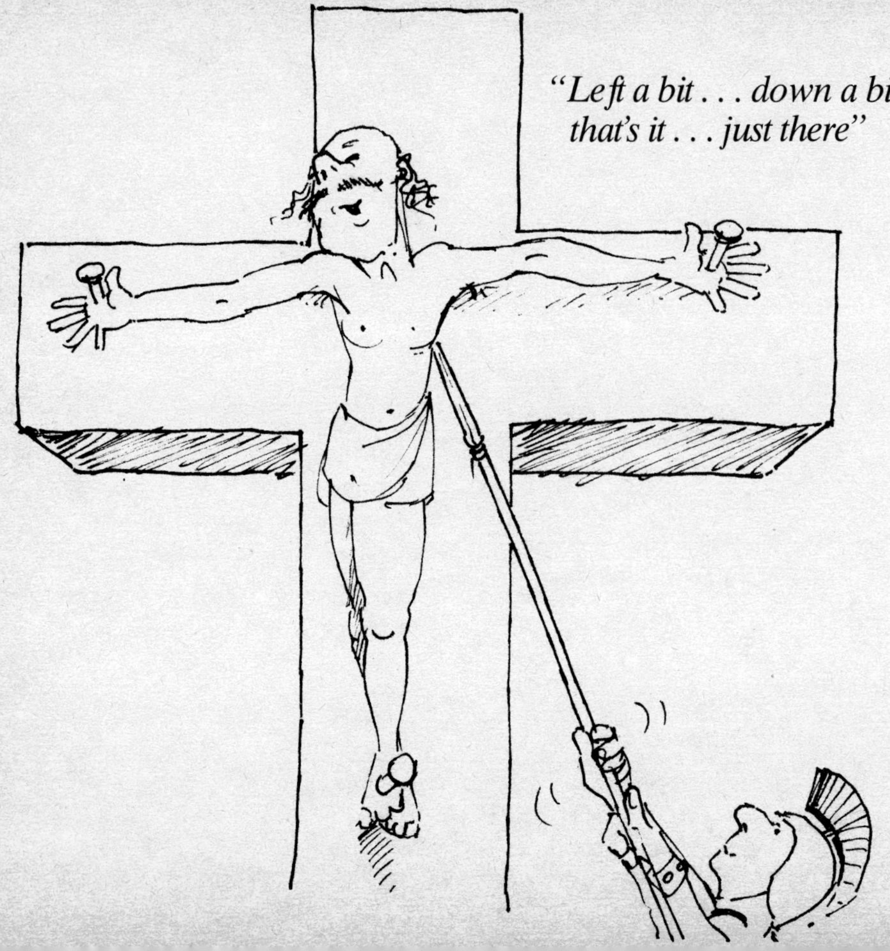

"Left a bit . . . down a bit . . . up a bit . . . that's it . . . just there"

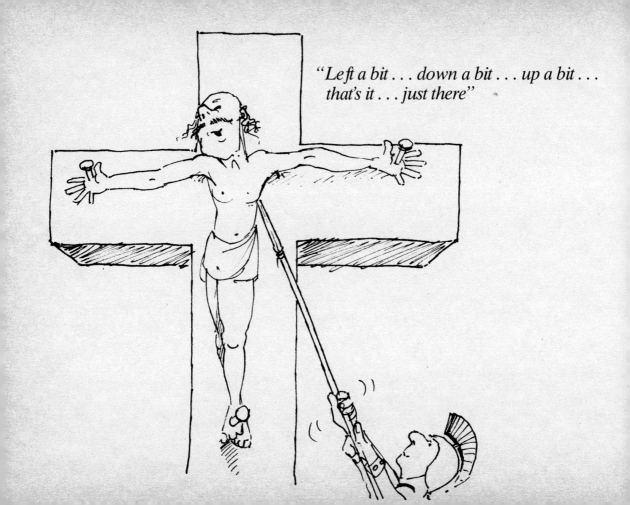

"Well, well . . . who'd have believed it?"

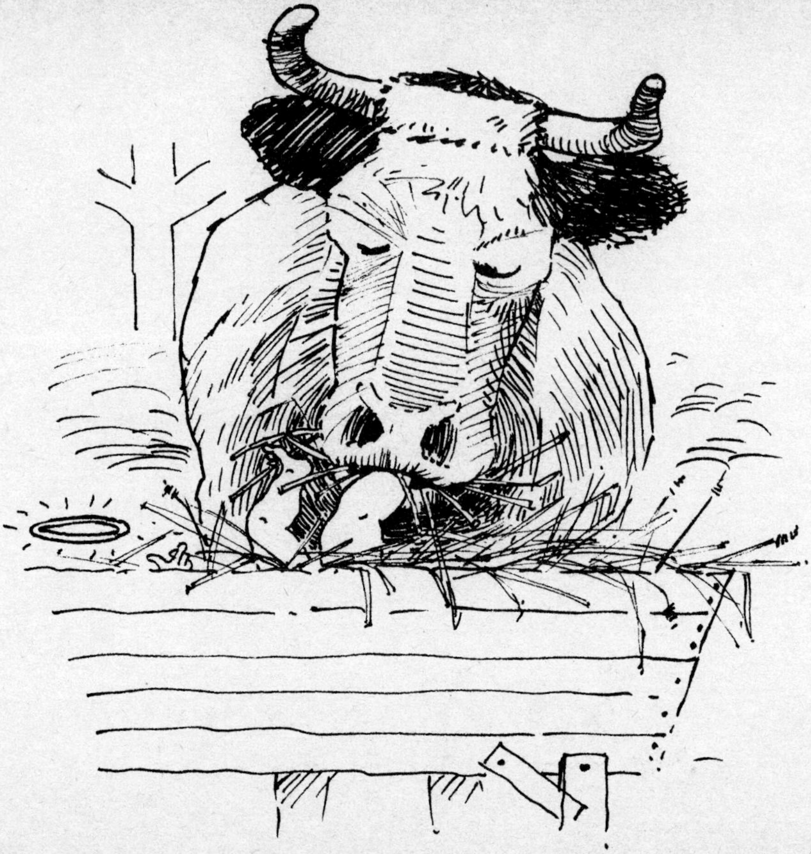

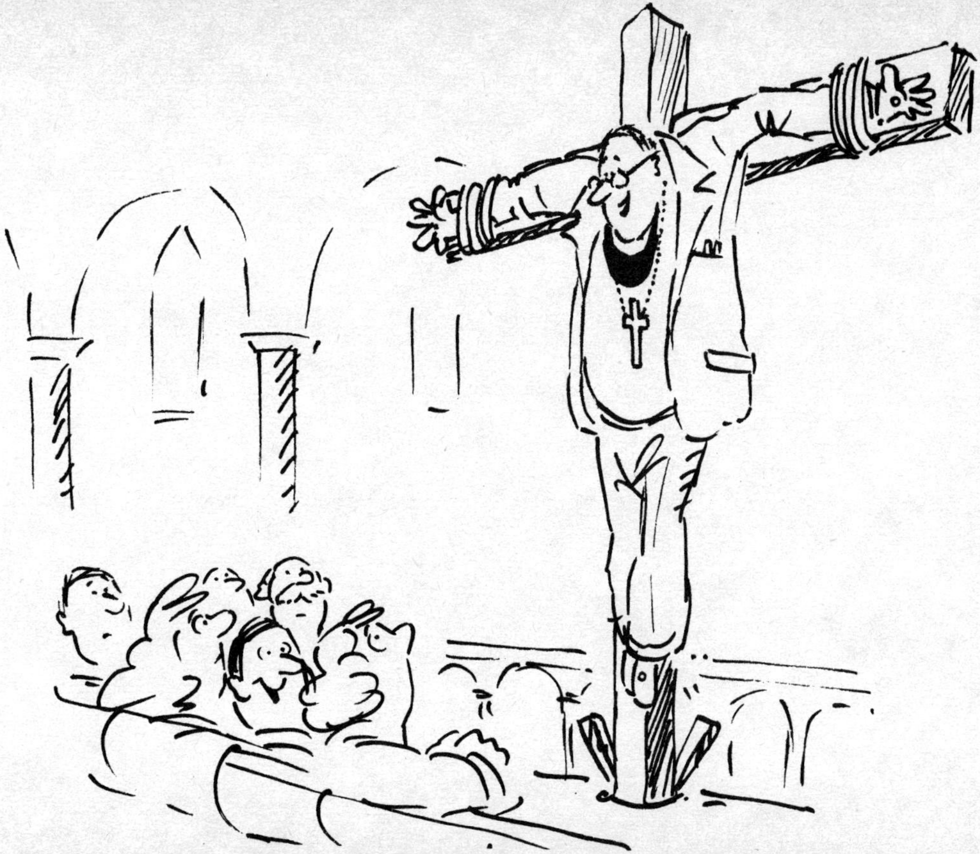

"He certainly gets his message over doesn't he?"

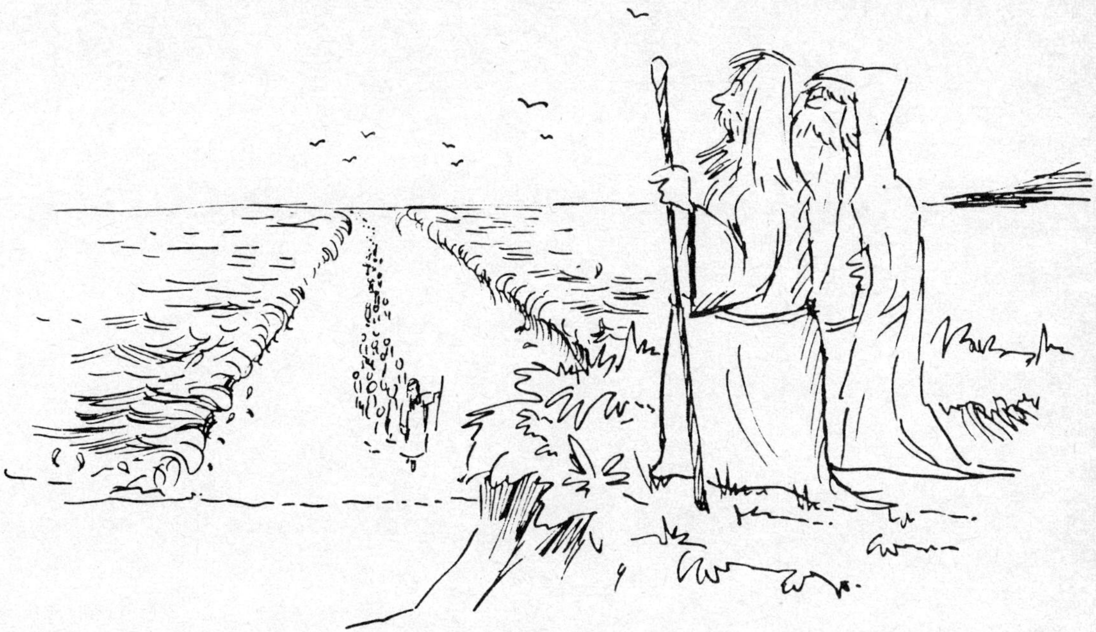

"I tell you, people today have got it too easy"

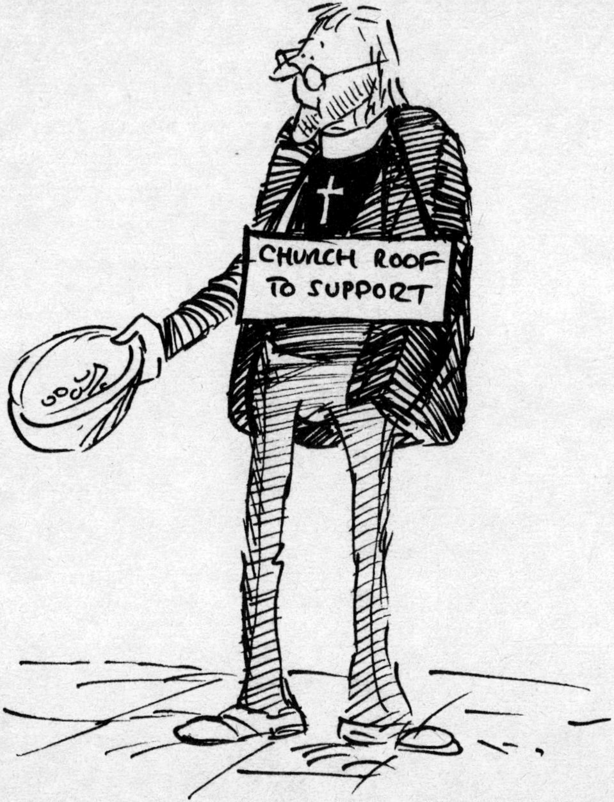
CHURCH ROOF
TO SUPPORT

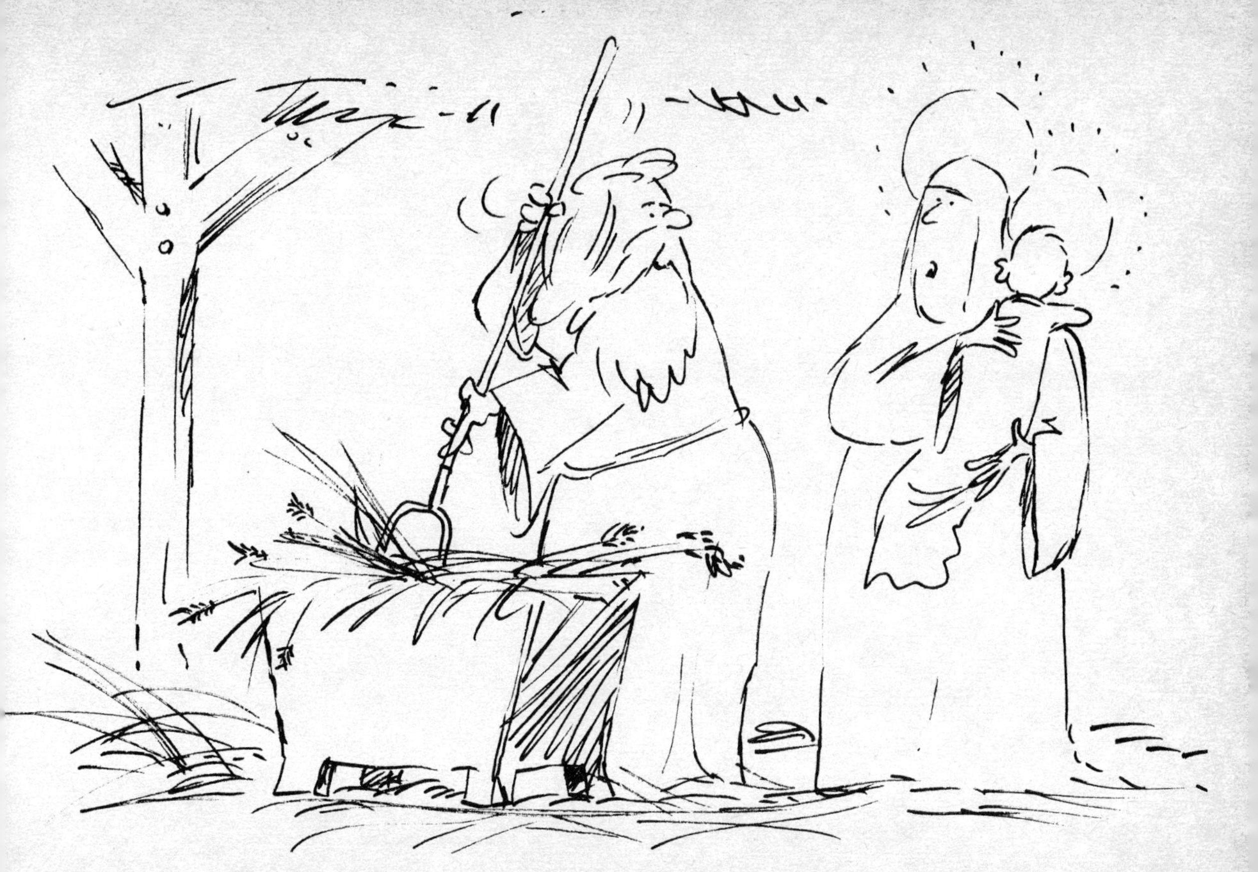

"That's why he was crying – his straw needed changing"

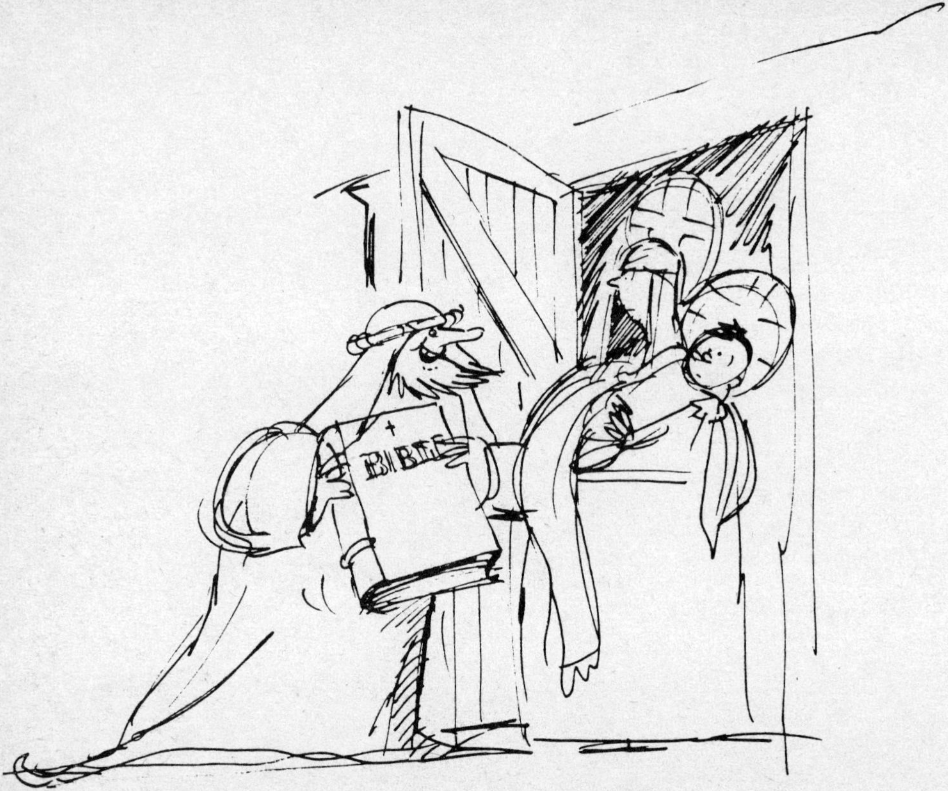
BIBLE

"Good Morning Madam . . . I wonder if I could interest you in . . ."

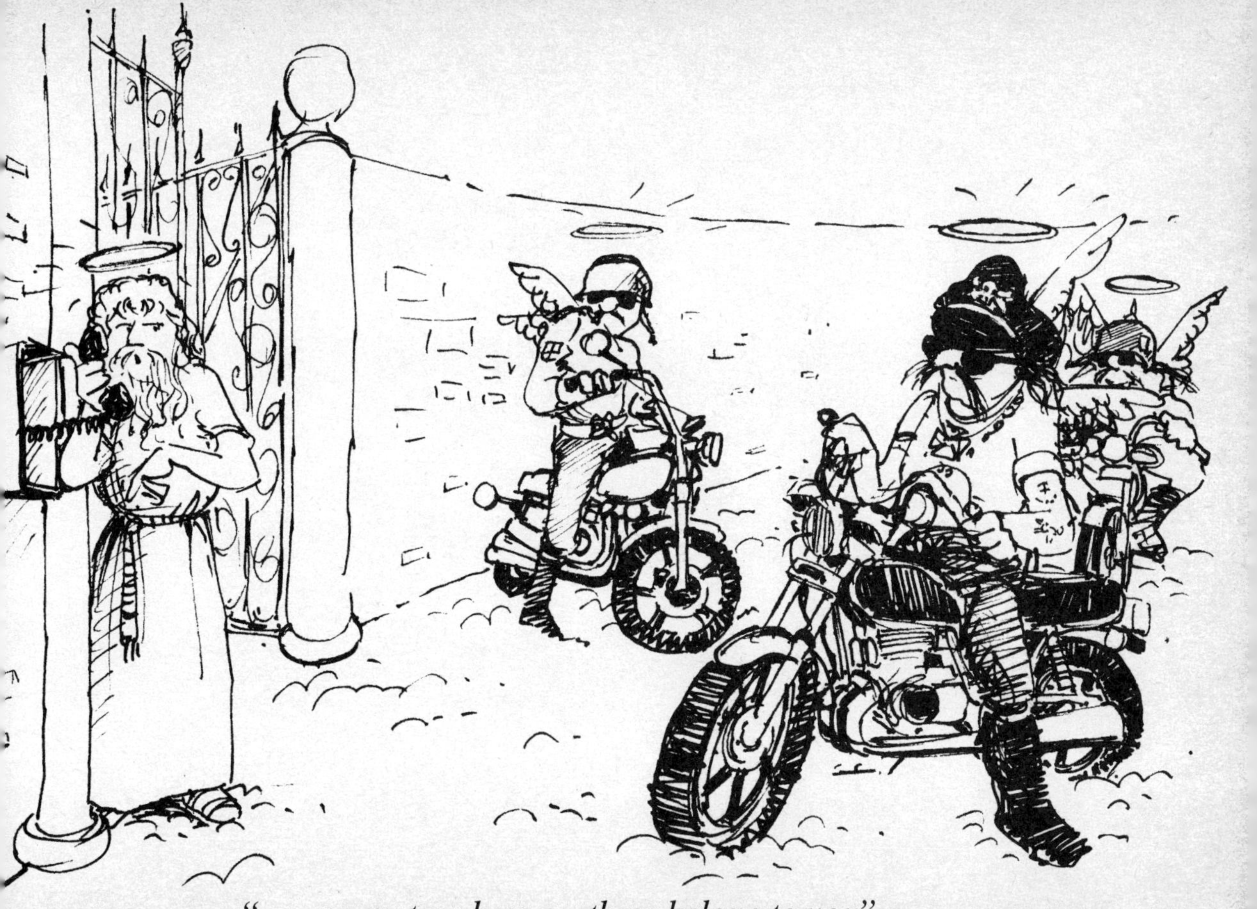

". . . no, not up here . . . these belong to you"

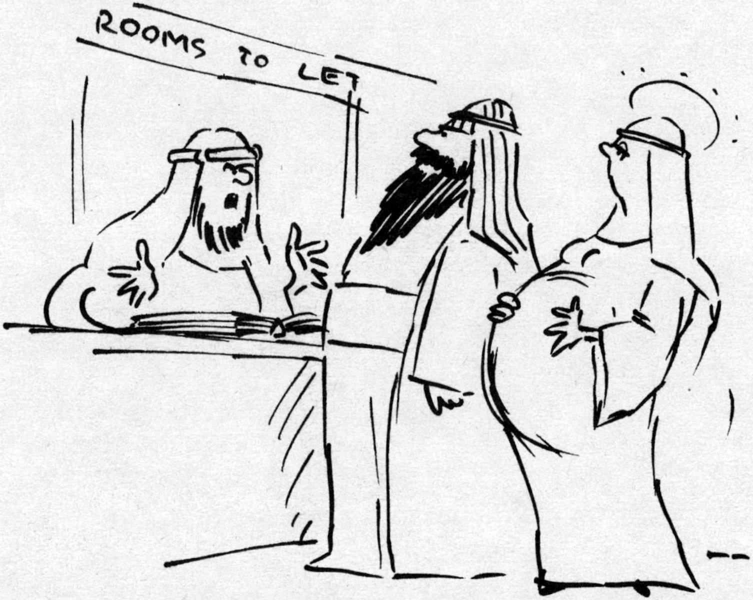
ROOMS TO LET

"Well if you can't write your name – put a cross"

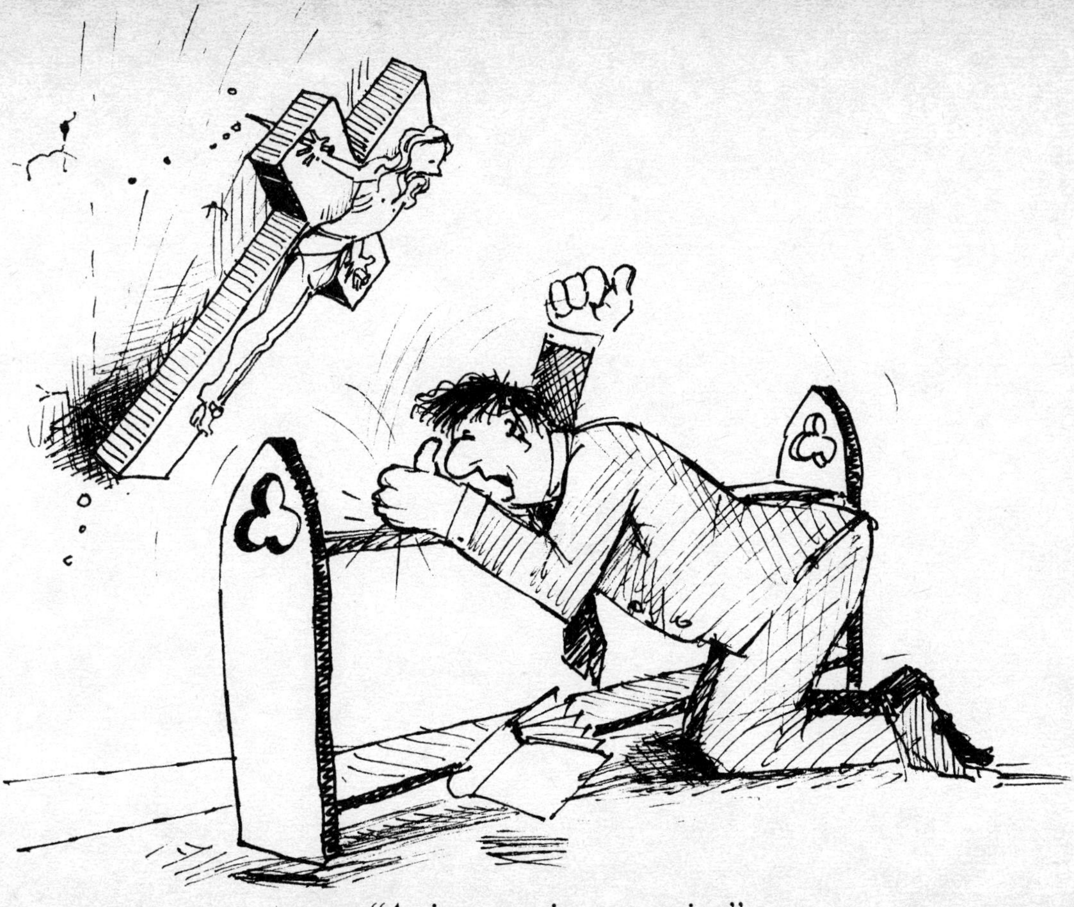

"A sign . . . give me a sign"

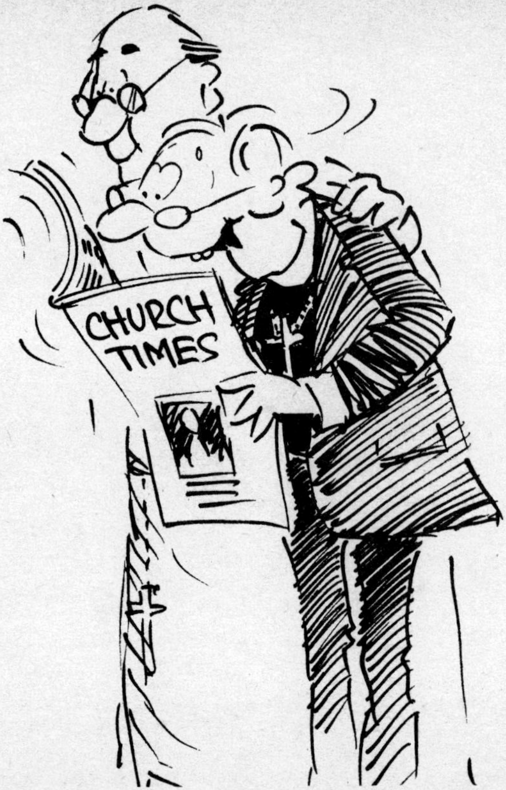
CHURCH
TIMES

"Look Bishop – Sister Ruth has made Page Three"

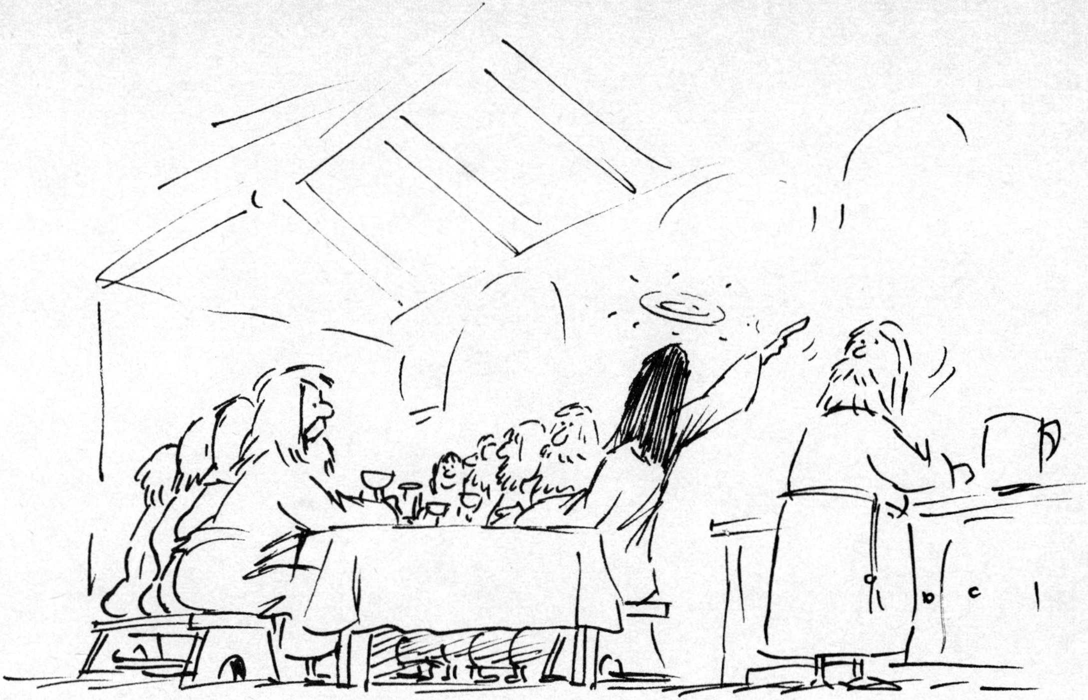

"Coffee and the bill please"

“. . .and there were two fishes, this big I tell you”

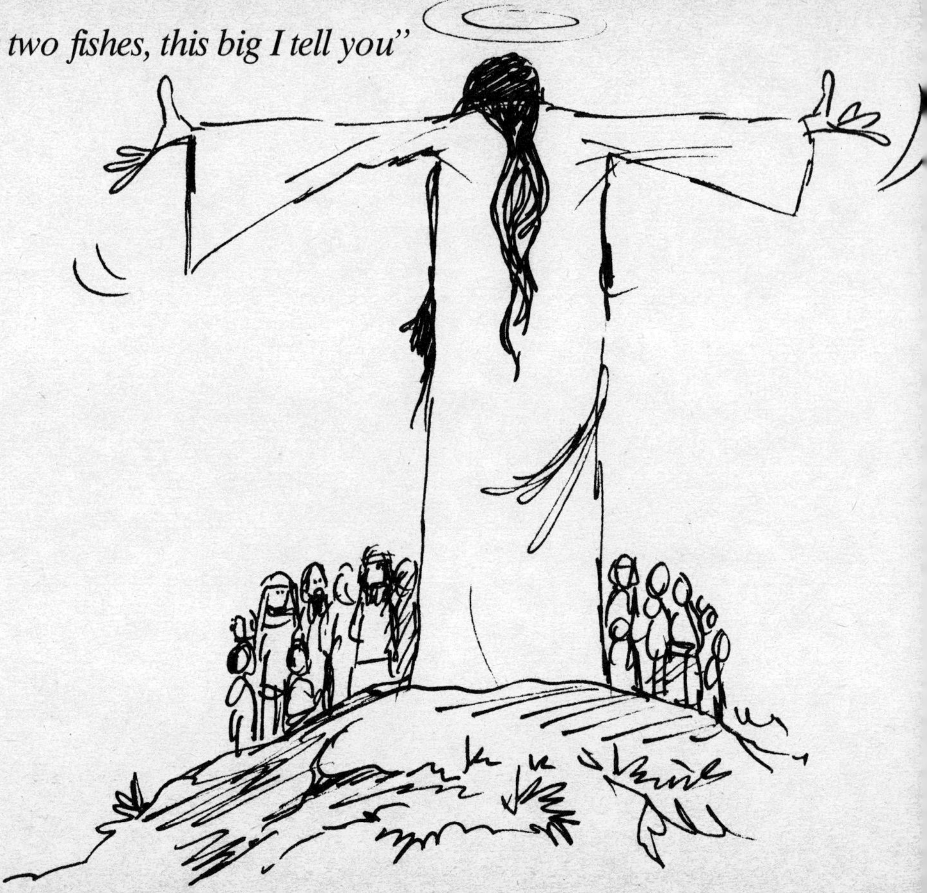

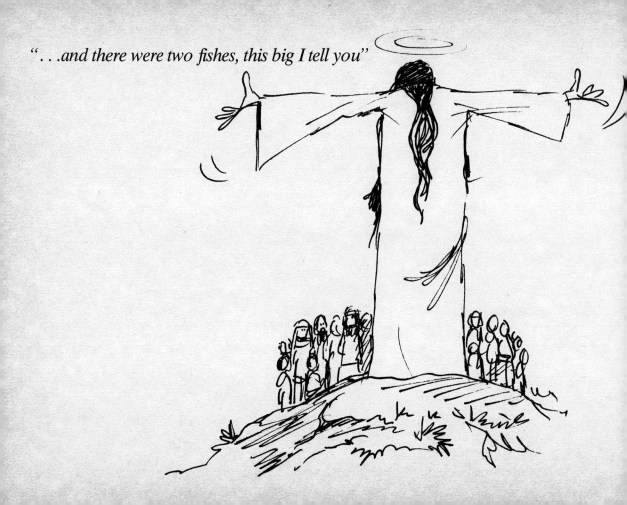

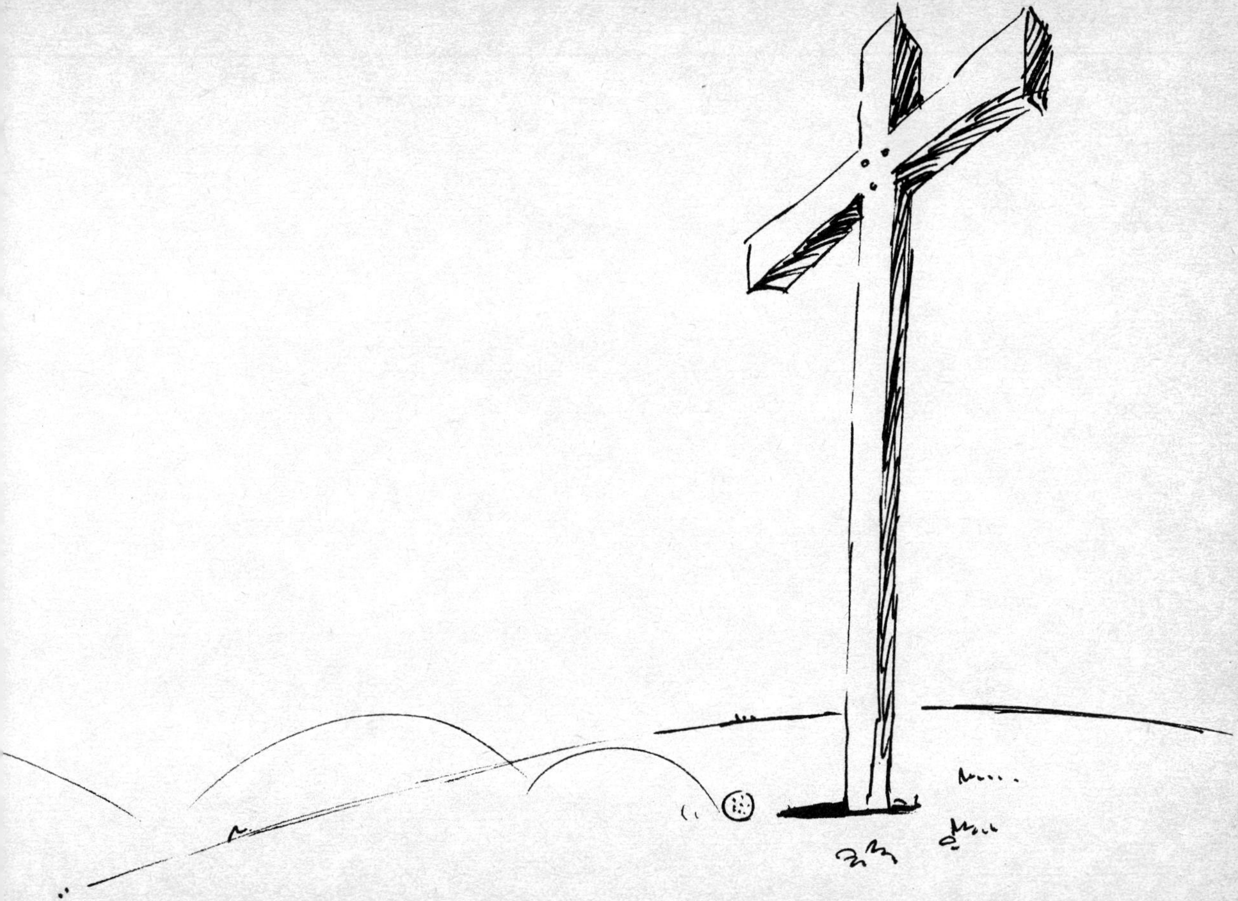

"Oh you bring out the worst in me, you devil"

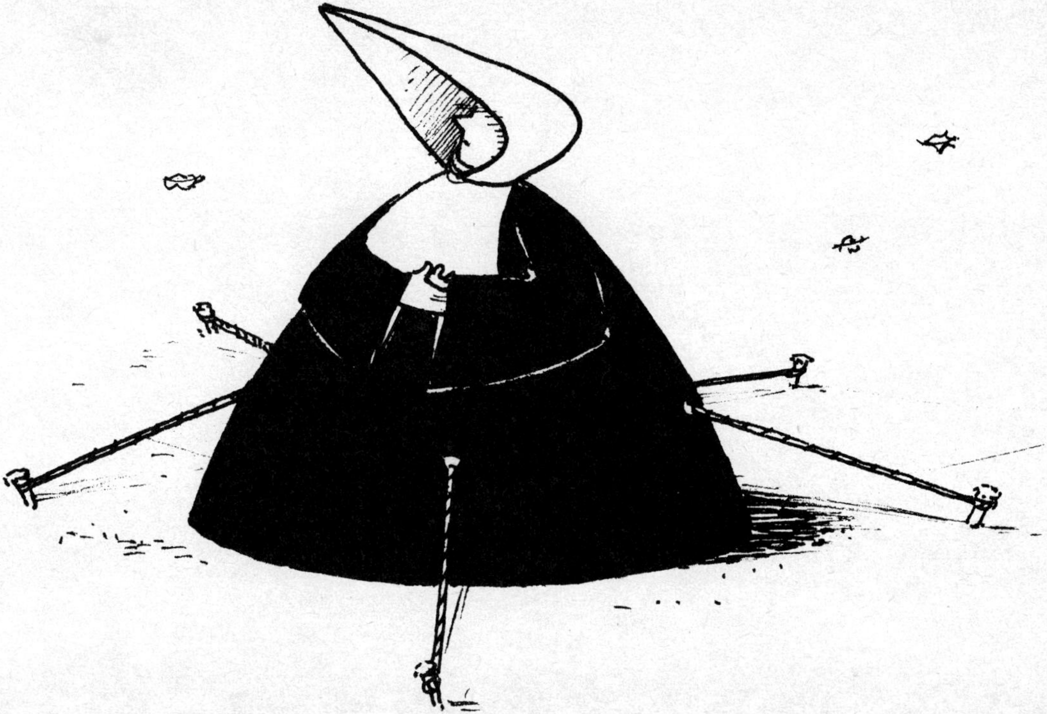

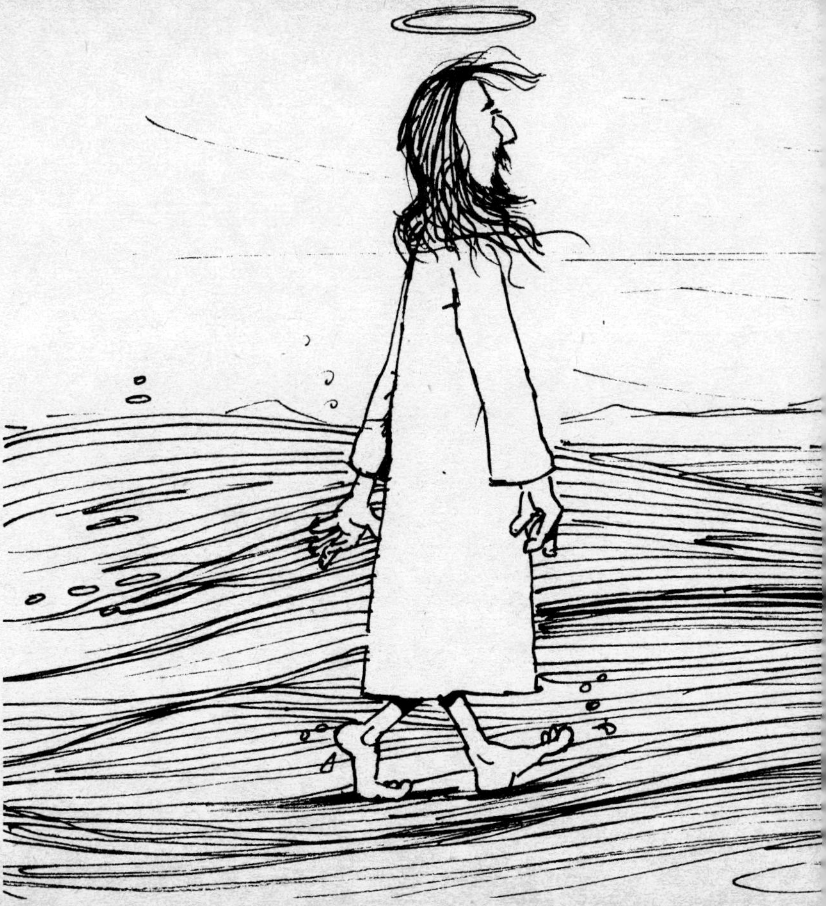

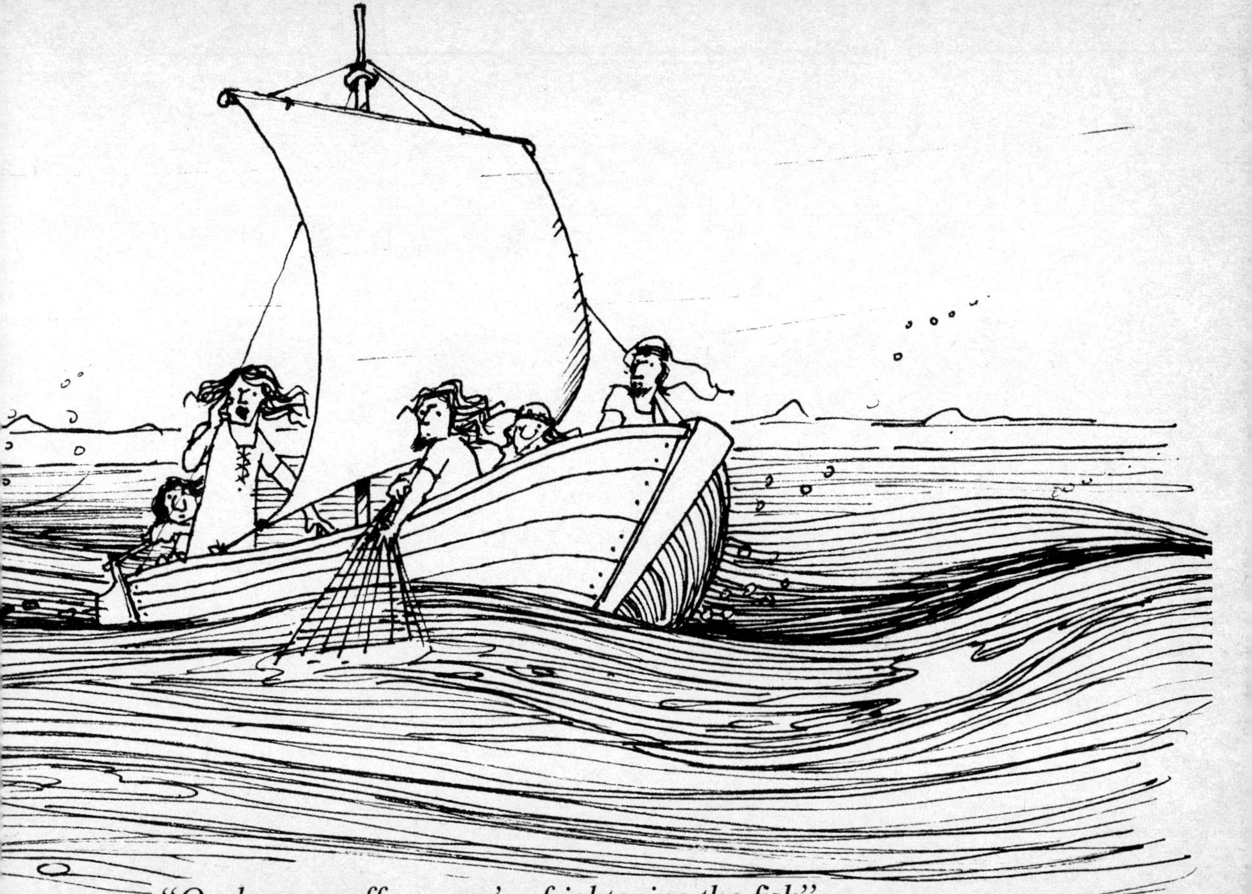

"Oy, bugger off . . . you're frightening the fish"

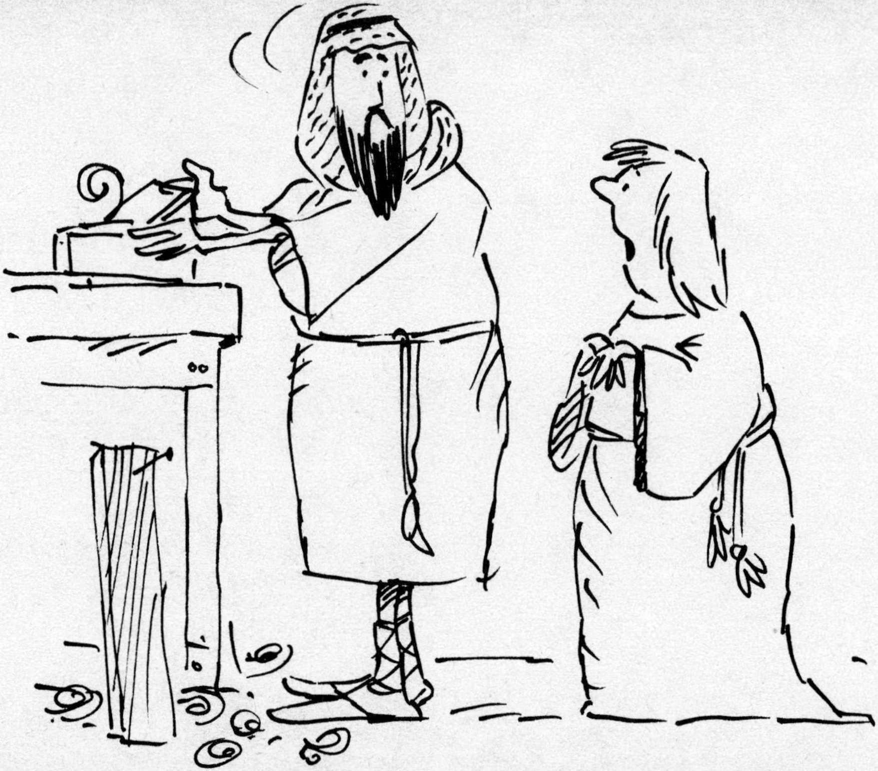

"Joseph. Your vasectomy didn't work"

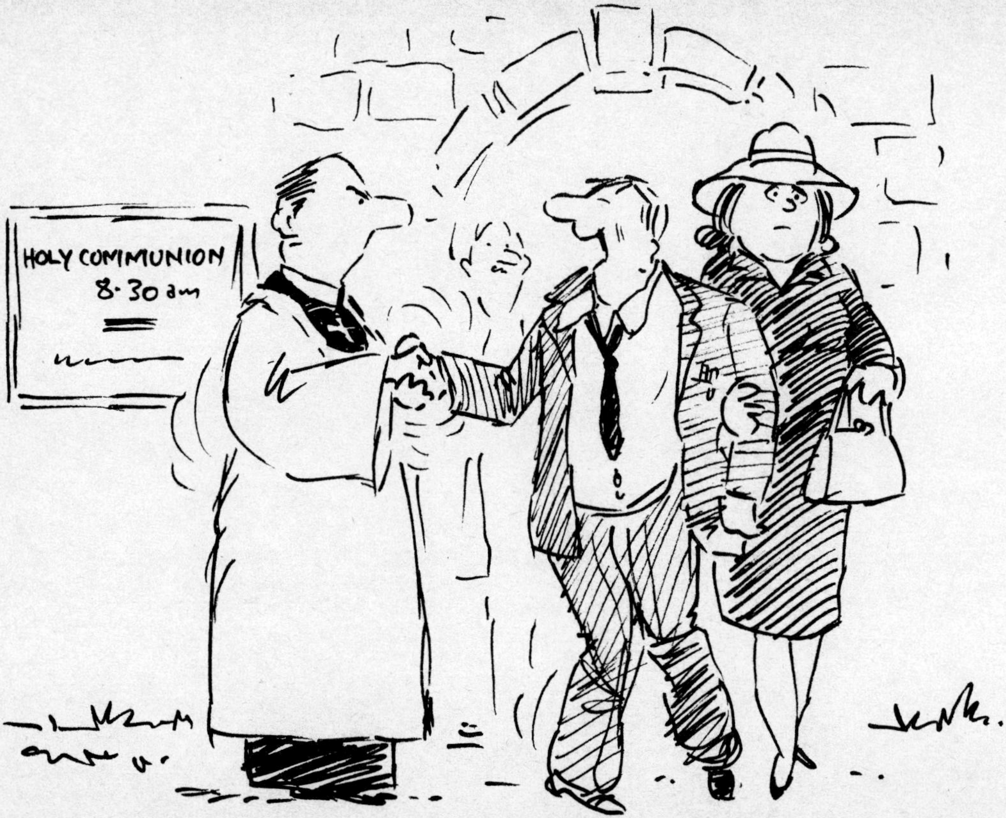
HOLY COMMUNION
8·30 am

"T'riffic sermon Vicar . . . and ta very much for the drink"

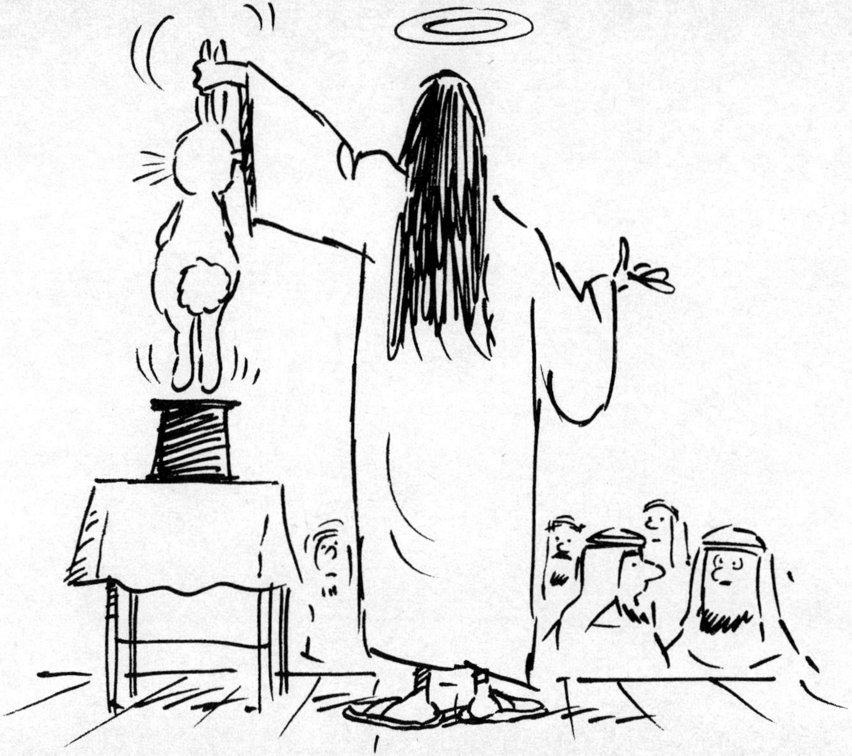

"Not quite the kind of miracle I was expecting"

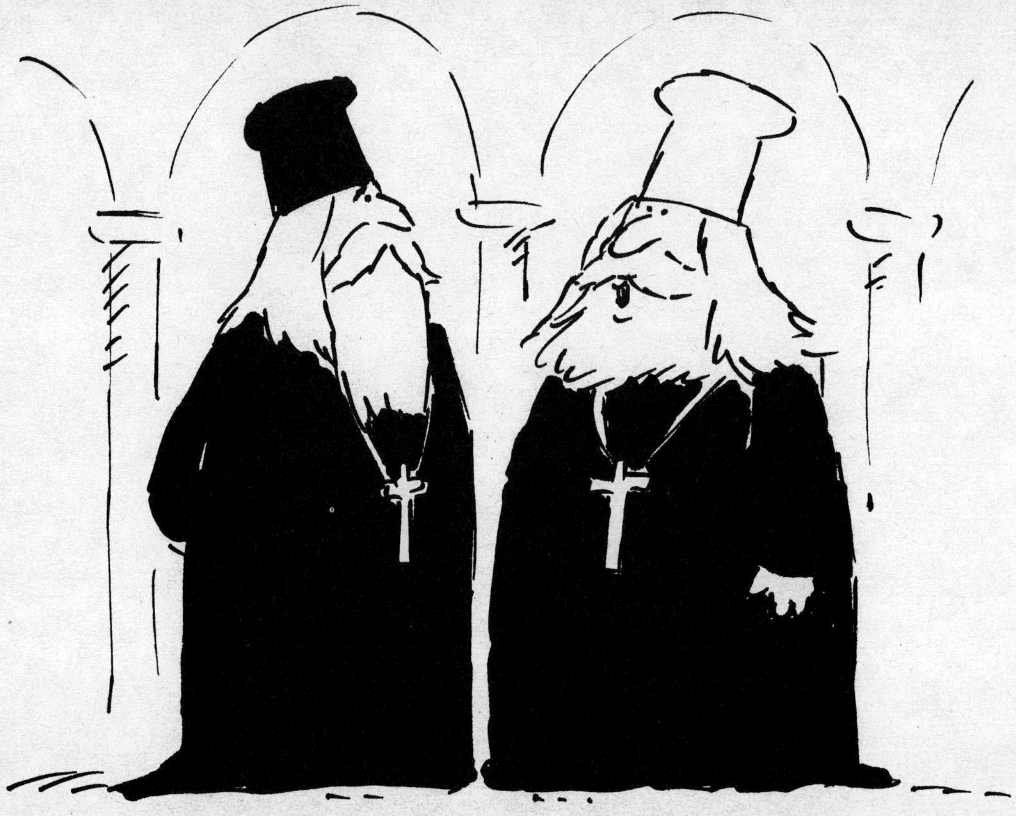

"Good Morning Archbishop, I'm the new chef"

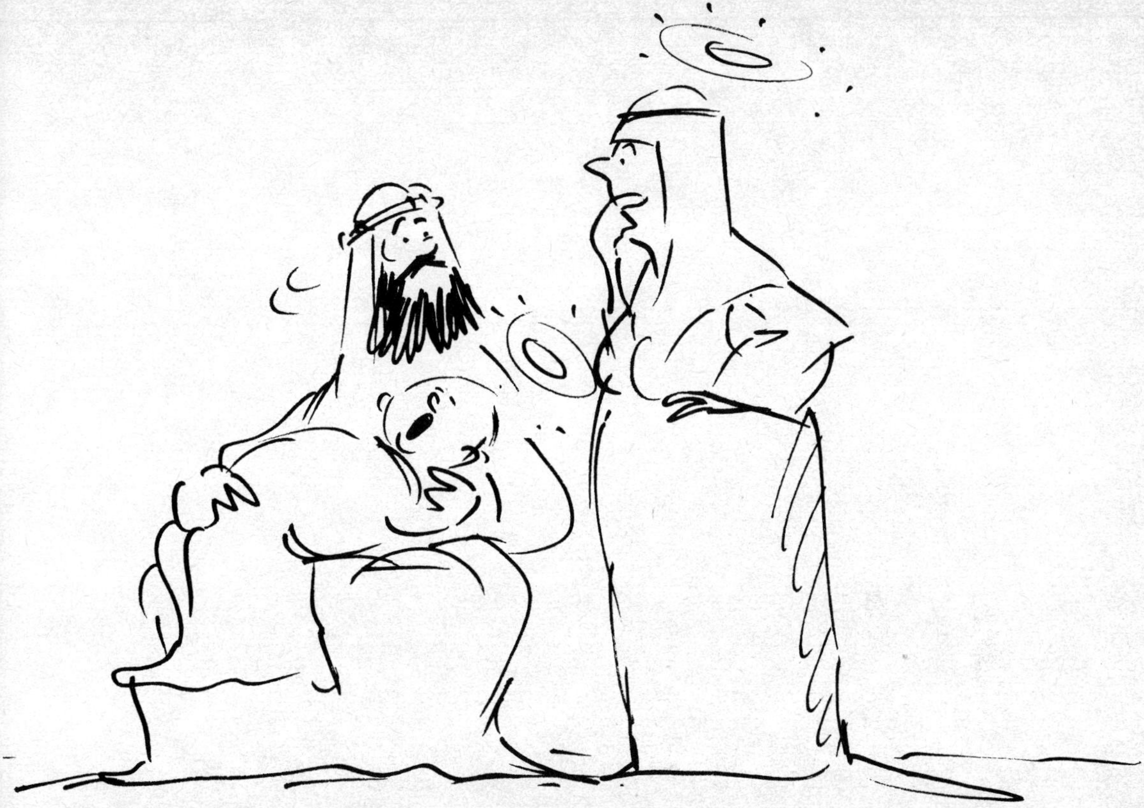

"We'll have to keep it quiet Joseph . . . I'm pregnant again"

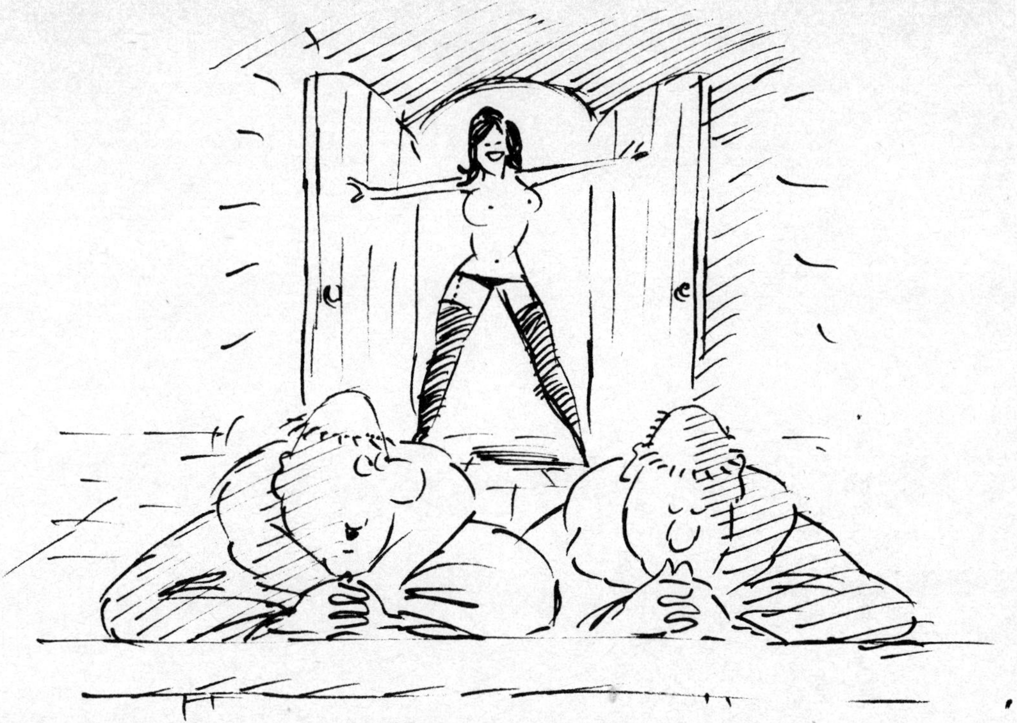

"Don't look now Brother, but I think our prayers have just been answered"

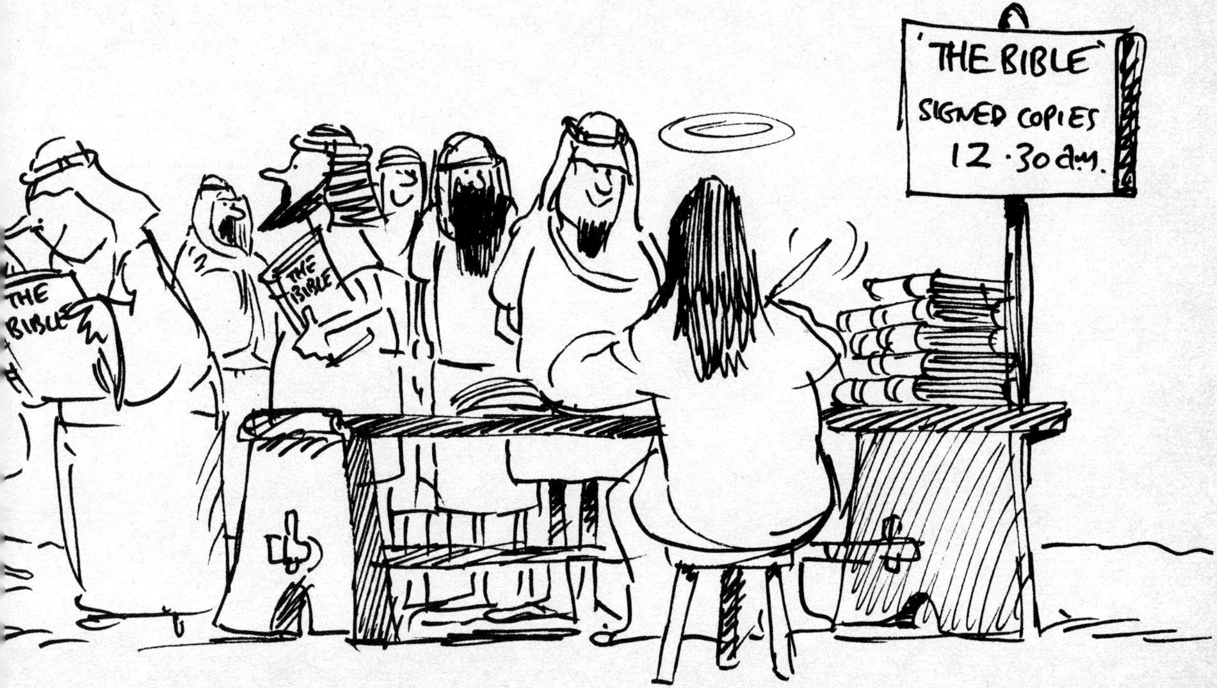
'THE BIBLE'
SIGNED COPIES
12·30 a.m.
THE BIBLE
THE BIBLE

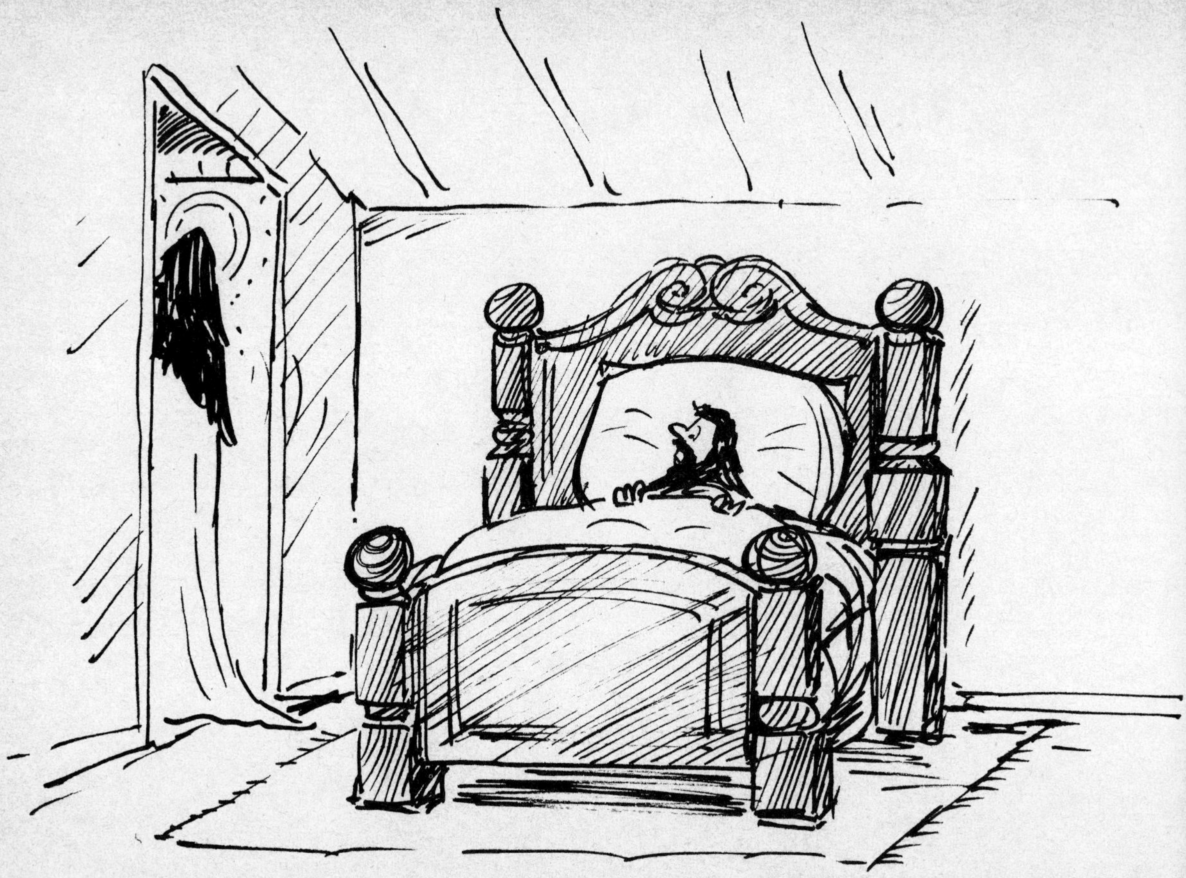

"Pick up thy bed and walk?"

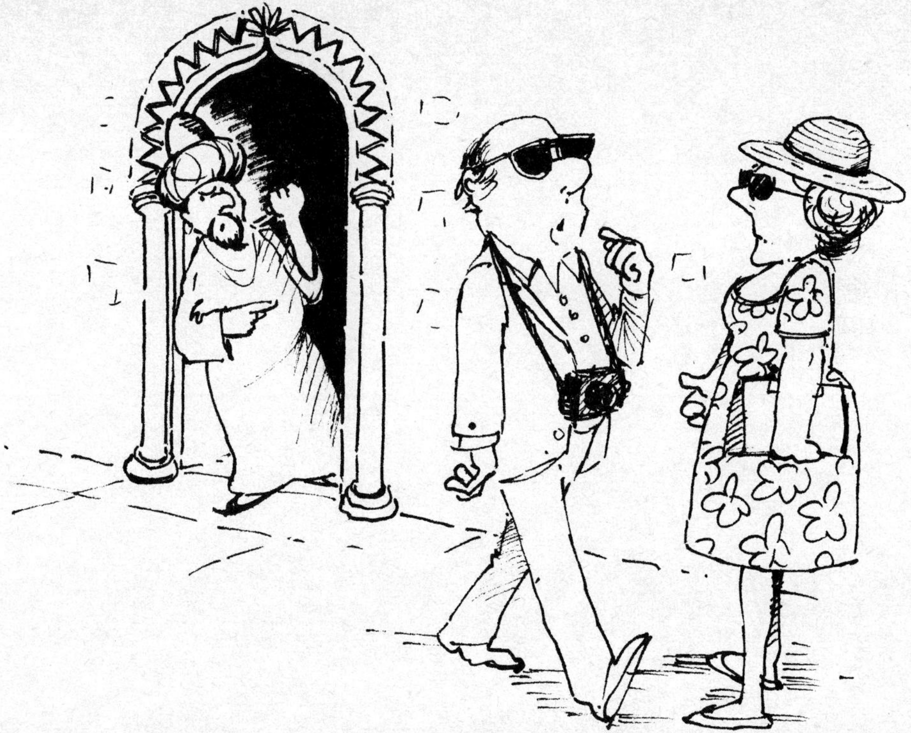

"Apparently, I wiped my feet on his prayer mat"

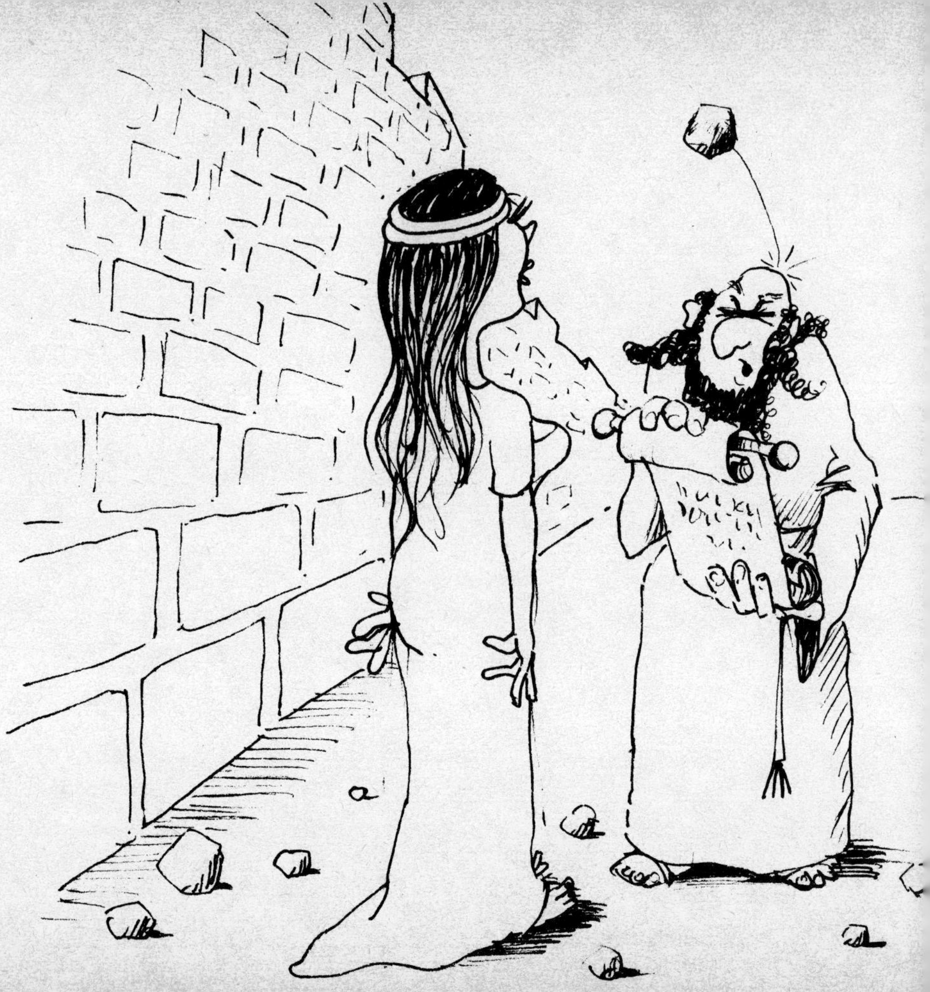

"They can't wait, some of 'em"

"I think it's wearing black that makes us so bloody miserable"

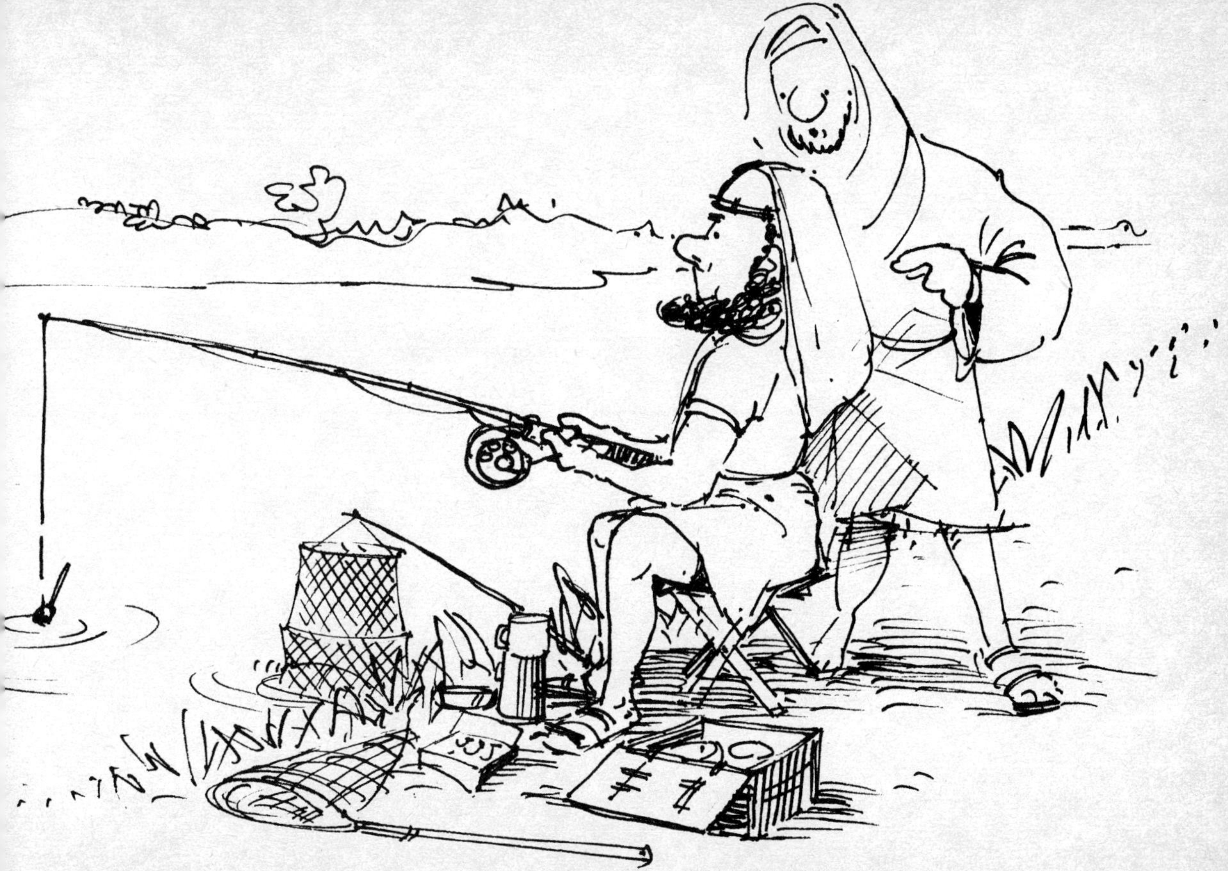

"Um . . . Peter the Fisherman?"

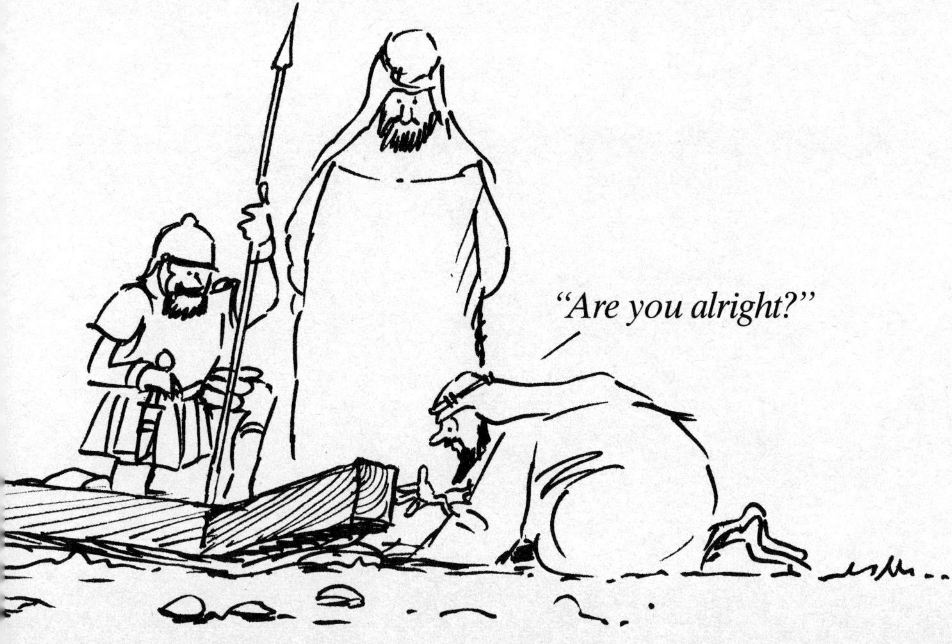
"Are you alright?"

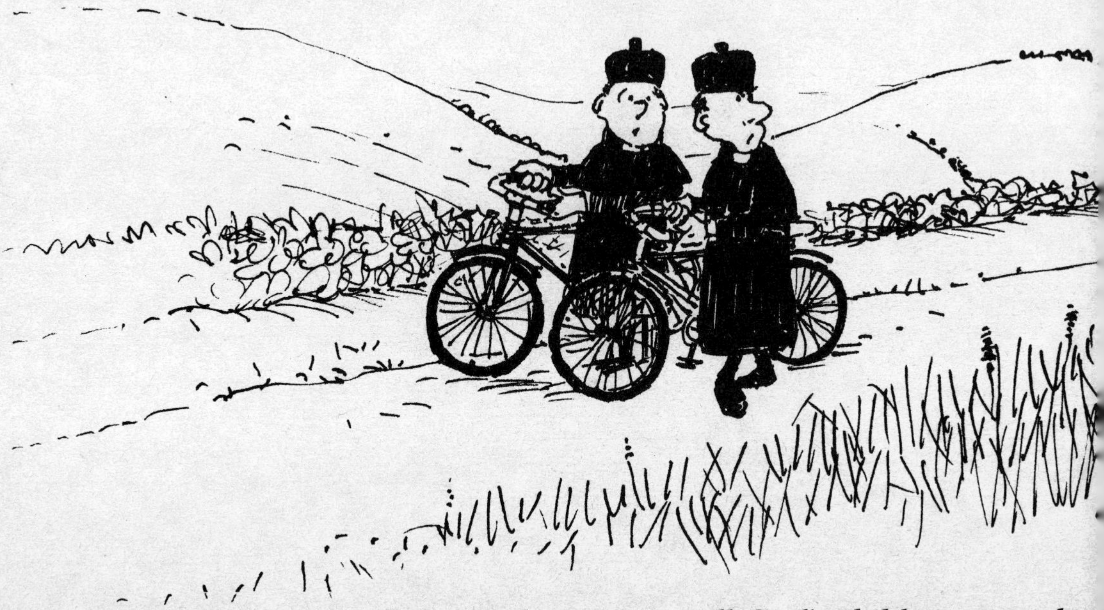

"Alas Father, it seems all God's children got rythm

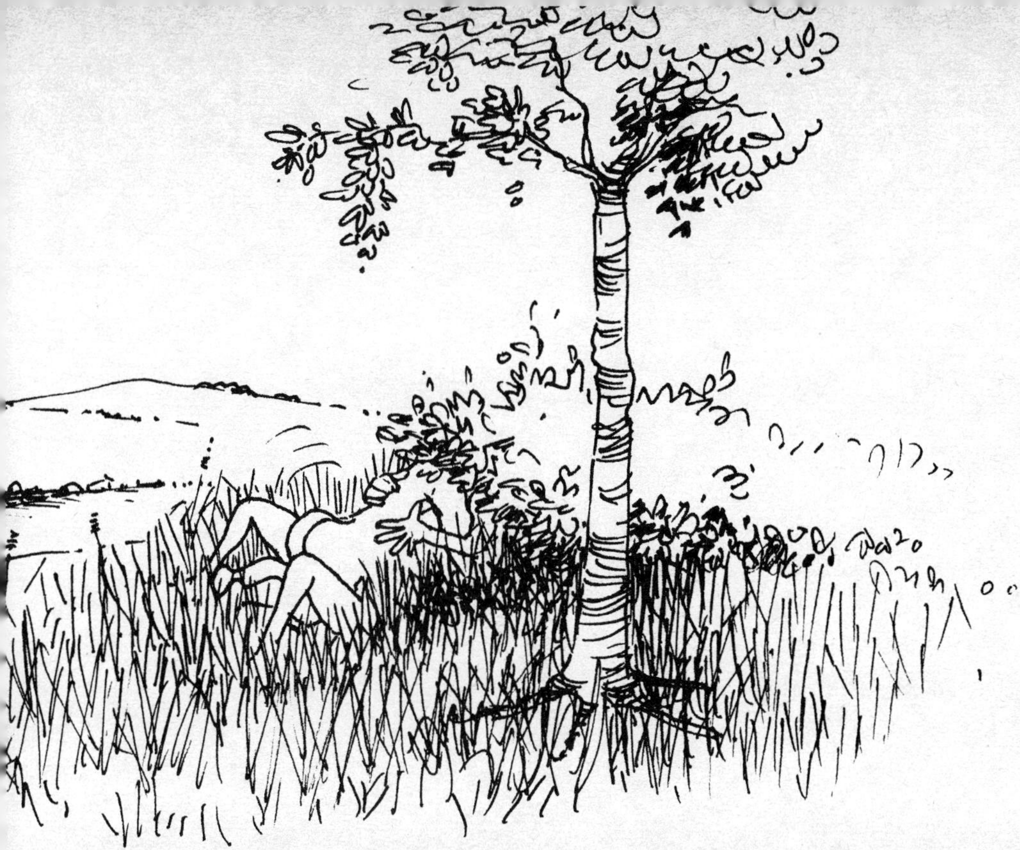

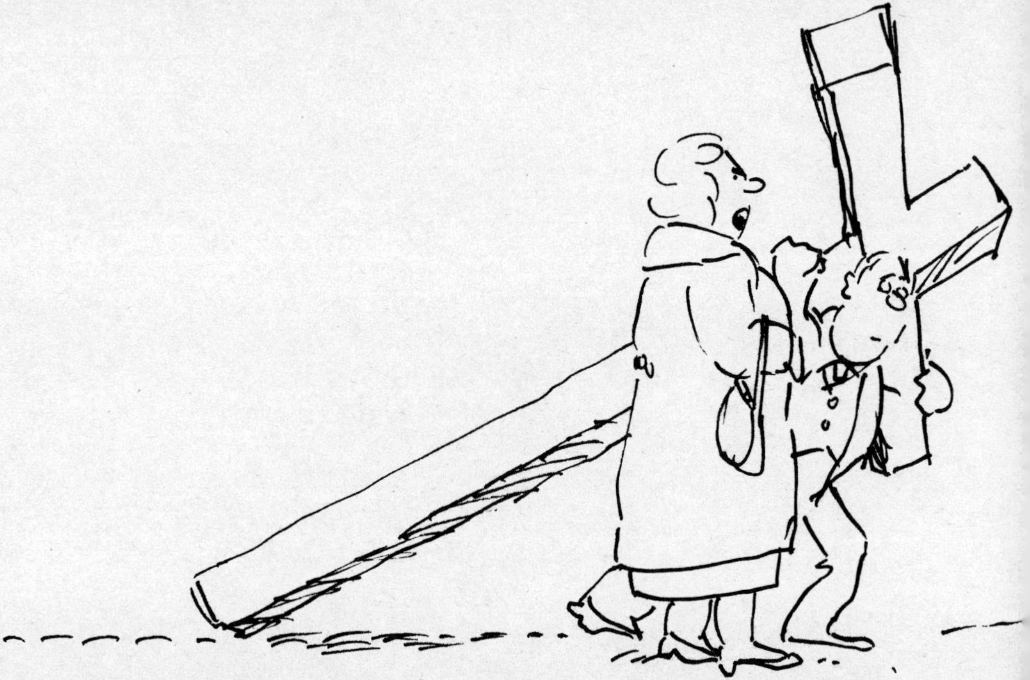

"I do wish you wouldn't patronize the vicar so muc

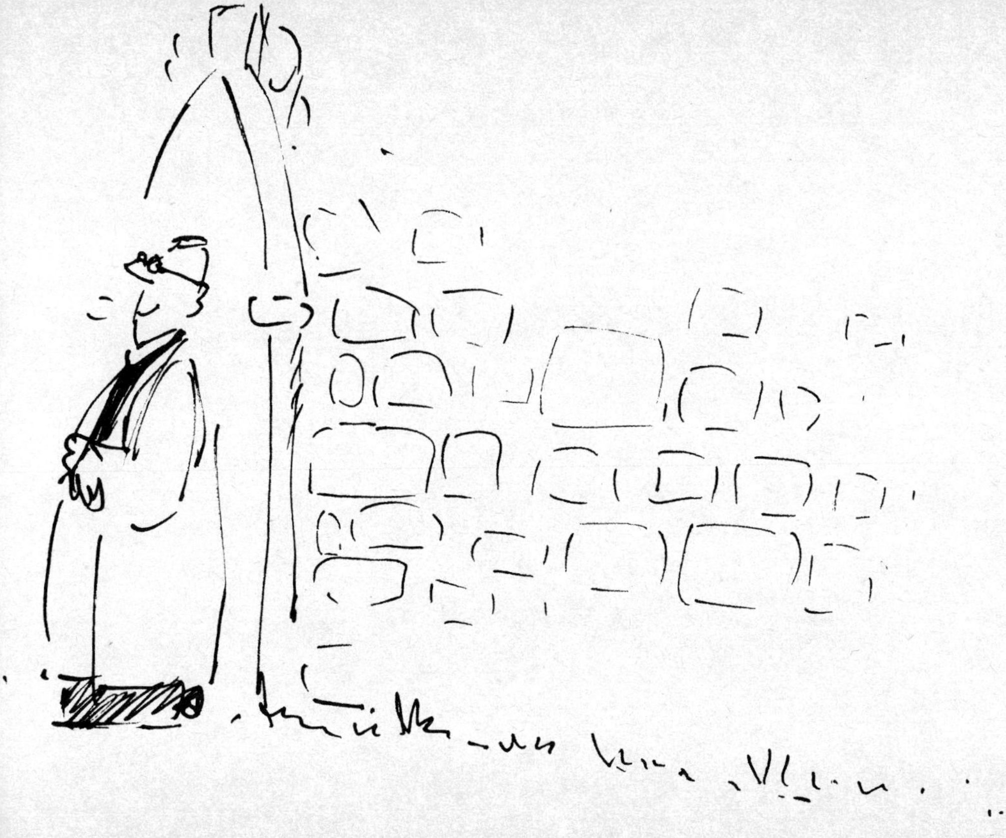

"It must be a message from God"

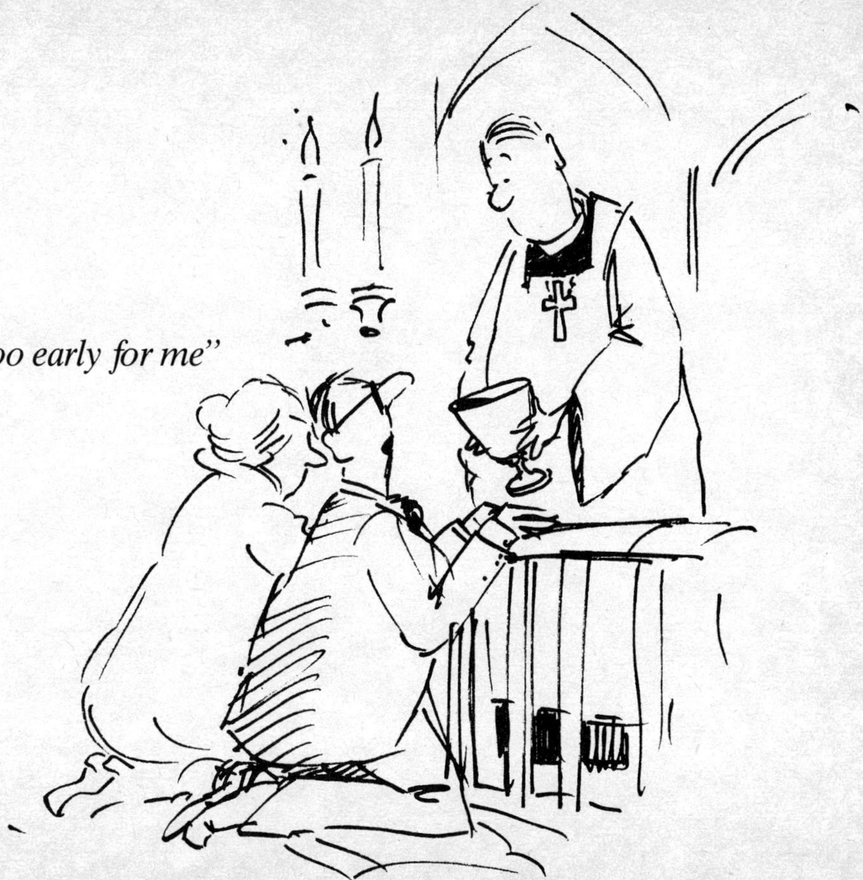

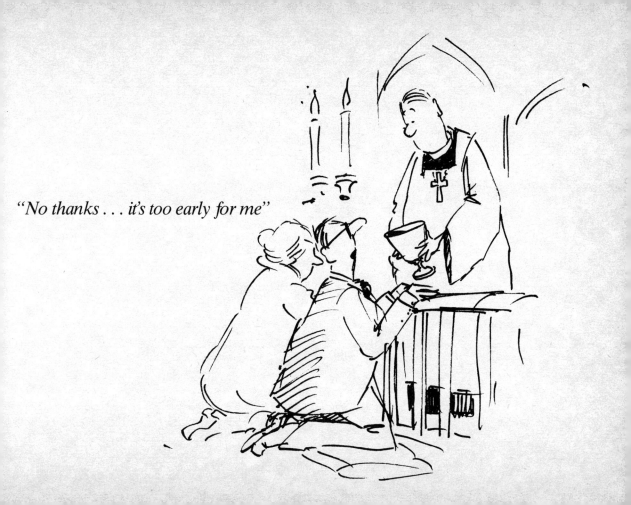

"No thanks . . . it's too early for me"

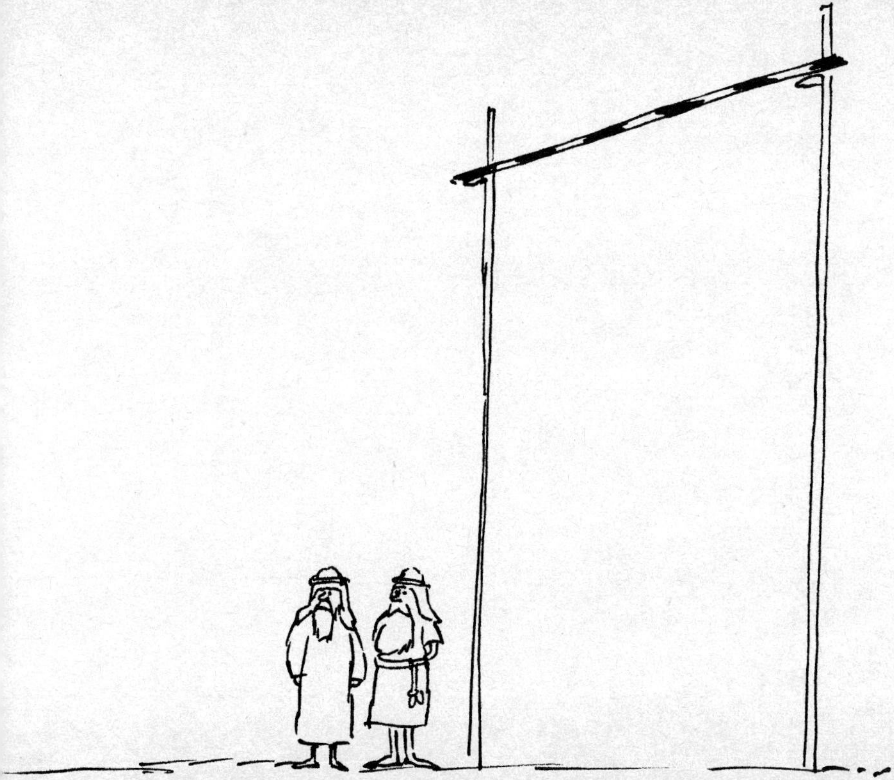

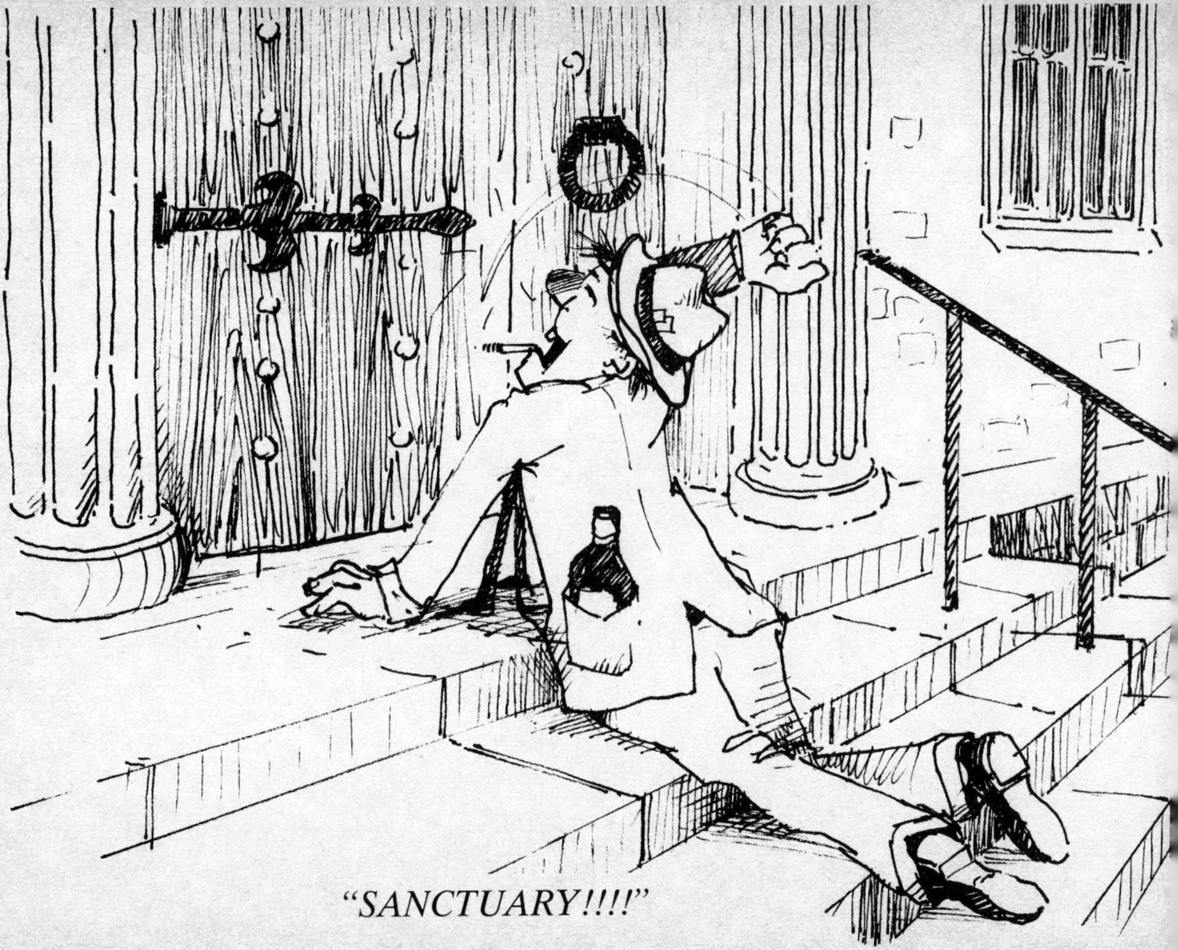

"SANCTUARY!!!!"

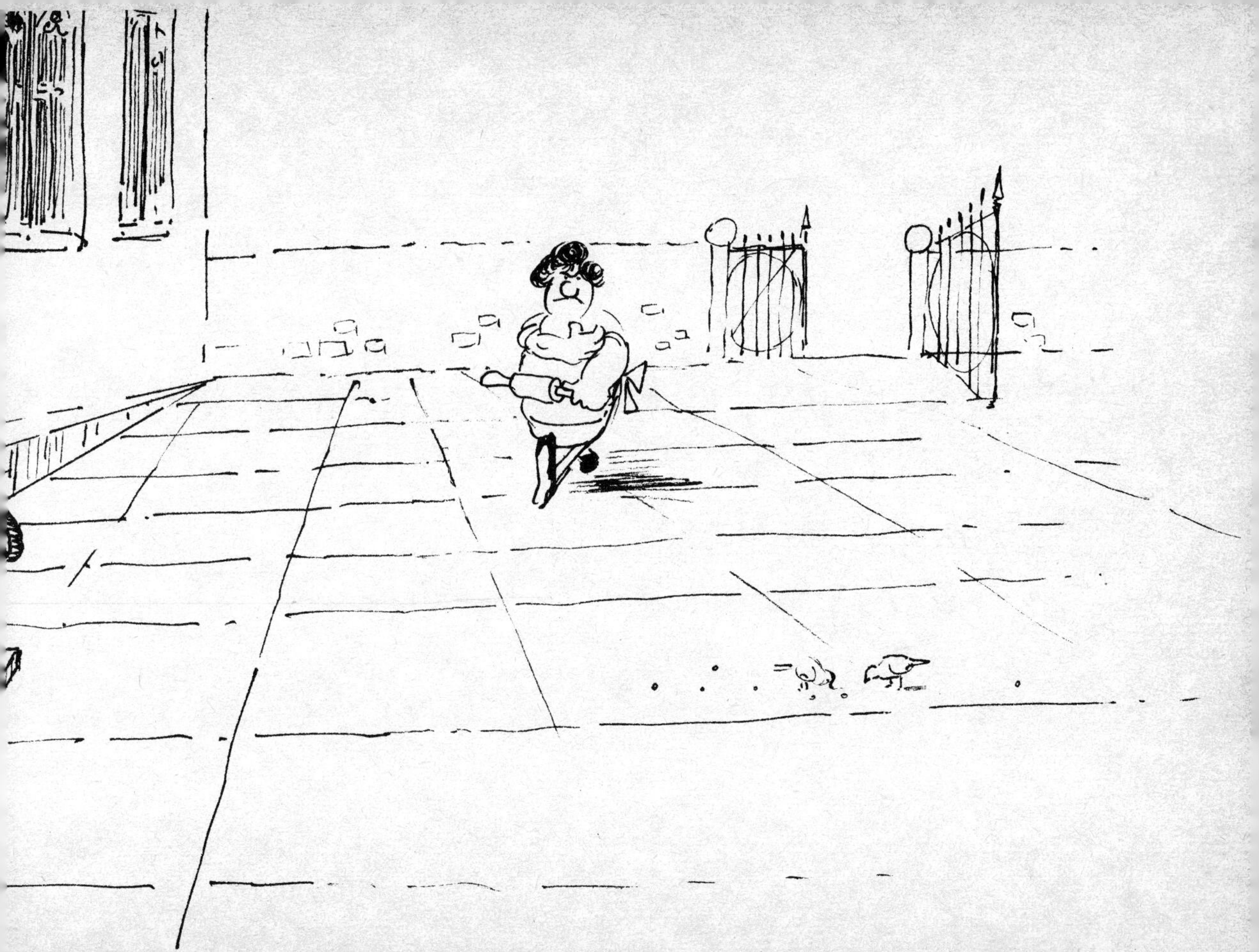

*"Well . . . as I said to the actress
. . . lets' get these
    bloody clothes off"*

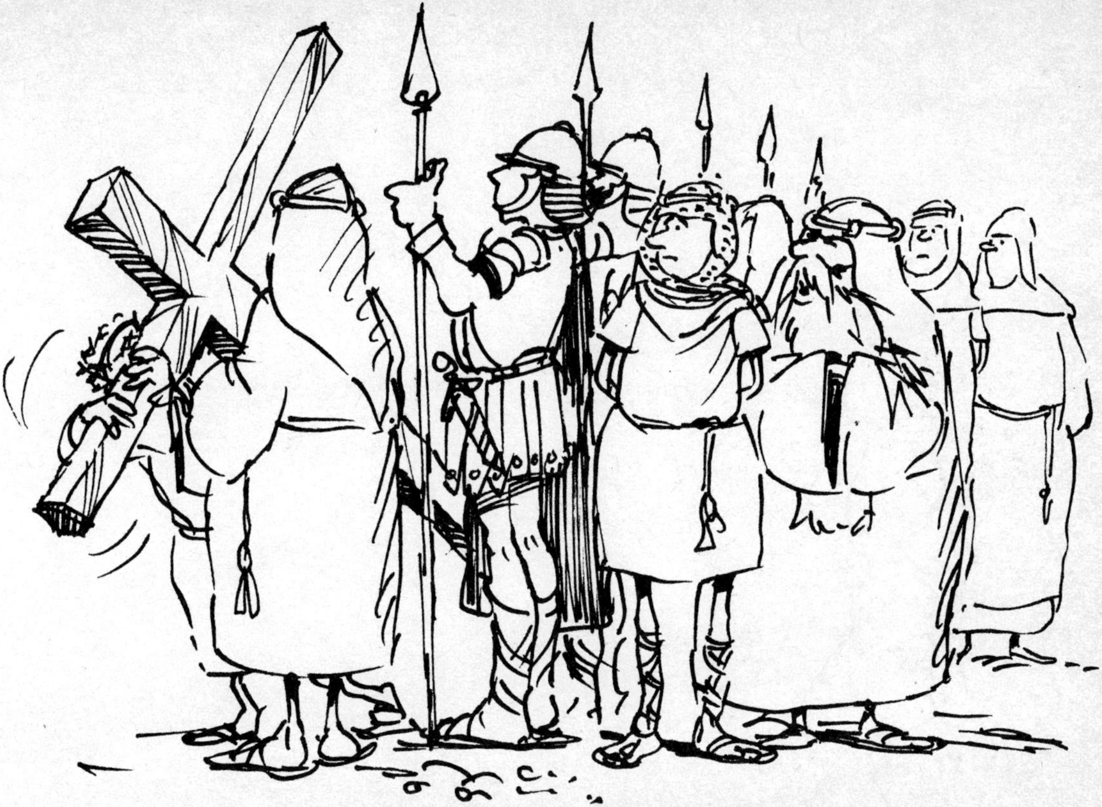

"Well . . . we all have our crosses to bear, you know"

Also published by Silvey-Jex Publications
BAD TASTE BOOKS
including
TOILET HUMOUR, GERIATRICS, ILLNESS, BOGIES.
TOILET HUMOUR NO 2, WILDLIFE, SNOWMEN, FLASHERS.
CHRISTMAS
BAD TASTE FROM BEGINNING TO END

BOY AND GIRL

SNAILSBURY TALES